THE ULTIMATE WINNING MINDS QUIZ CHALLENGE

Derek O'Brien was born in Kolkata. He began his career as a journalist for *Sportsworld* magazine but soon shifted to advertising. After working for a number of very successful years as Creative Head of Oglivy, Derek decided to focus all his energy and talent in his passion—quizzing.

Today, Derek is Asia's best-known quizmaster and the CEO of Derek O'Brien & Associates. He is the host of the longest-running game show on Indian television, the Cadbury Bournvita Quiz Contest, for which he was voted the Best Anchor of a Game Show at the Indian Television Academy Awards for three years in a row. Always innovating, Derek is also credited with having conducted the first quiz on Twitter in 2010.

Derek has written over fifty bestselling reference, quiz and textbooks. In 2011, he was voted to the Rajya Sabha as a Member of Parliament (MP) and is the Leader of the Trinamool Congress Parliamentary Party in the Rajya Sabha.

Other books by Derek O'Brien
(published by Rupa Publications)

Bournvita Quiz Contest Quiz Book 2012

The Ultimate BQC Book of Knowledge (Volumes 1 and 2)

The Best of BQC

Derek's Challenge

Speak Up, Speak Out: My Favourite Elocution Pieces and How to Deliver Them

My Way: Success Mantras of 12 Achievers

Derek Introduces: 100 Iconic Indians

Bournvita Quiz Contest Quiz Book 2014

BQC Quiz Book 3

Bumper BQC Quiz Book

THE ULTIMATE WINNING MINDS QUIZ CHALLENGE

DEREK O' BRIEN

RUPA

Published by
Rupa Publications India Pvt. Ltd 2016
161-B/4, Gulmohar House,
Yusuf Sarai Community Centre,
New Delhi 110049

Sales centres:
Bengaluru Chennai
Hyderabad Kolkata Mumbai

P-ISBN: 978-81-291-4235-1
E-ISBN: 978-81-291-4670-0

Second impression 2026

10 9 8 7 6 5 4 3 2

Printed in India

INTRODUCTION

In the 1960s, quizzes were held in small halls and clubs across some cities in India. In the 1970s, quizzing became extremely popular on the radio, with the Sayani brothers, first Hamid and then Ameen, hosting the *Bournvita Quiz Contest* every Sunday morning on Vividh Bharti. One of the fondest memories of my childhood is that of my parents sitting around the radio with my two brothers and I enjoying this Sunday ritual.

Then came television, with Doordarshan, in the 1980s, airing popular programmes like Siddhartha Basu's *Quiz Time* and Dr Narottam Puri's *Sports Quiz*. Monopoly television gave way to the satellite TV boom in the 1990s and in 1994, the *Bournvita Quiz Contest* appeared in its new avatar as a television programme. The team at Derek O'Brien & Associates re-created this iconic quiz show for Zee TV and later Sony.

In 2000, Mr Amitabh Bachchan forever redefined the role of the quizmaster. *Kaun Banega Crorepati* moved quizzing from a niche pastime into a national obsession.

Then came the age of social media and social networking

sites. It was only a natural progression that quizzes would move there too. The Twitter quiz I started in 2010 is credited as the first quiz on Twitter in India. Since then, over the past six years, every Sunday at 11 a.m., we have been posting three questions on my Twitter handle @quizderek, with the lucky winner getting exciting prizes. The response has been wonderful and we have received answers from people and places as diverse as a middle-school student from Moradabad to an octogenarian from Singapore.

The Ultimate Winning Minds Quiz Challenge is a compilation of these questions.

Happy quizzing!

Derek O'Brien

P.S. You can follow me on Twitter at my handle @quizderek, or connect with me on Facebook at https://www.facebook.com/MPDerekOBrien.

WEEK 1

1. 'Industry, Impartiality and Integrity' is the motto of which Indian organization?
2. In an alphabetical list of state capitals of India, which city will appear on the top?
3. Who was the first Chairman of the Rajya Sabha?
4. Born on 10 January 1974, which actor is lovingly called 'Duggu' in the Hindi film industry?
5. The city of Allahabad is located at the confluence of three rivers: Ganga, Yamuna and the invisible____
6. In 1837, who became the first sovereign to take up residence in the Buckingham Palace?
7. ___ trading is the stock market trading activity for an hour on Diwali in India. Fill in the blank.
8. Which Indian Nobel Laureate was referred to as 'Zhu Zhen Dan' by most people in Haining, China?
9. Which scientist was appointed as an assistant at the Royal Institution by Humphry Davy in 1813?

10. Vasu Paranjape gave Sunil Gavaskar something that has stayed with Gavaskar forever. What was it?
11. Which was the first colour film to win an Oscar in the Best Picture category?
    a) *A Streetcar Named Desire*
    b) *Gone with the Wind*
    c) *A Midsummer Night's Dream*
    d) *Lawrence of Arabia*
12. Which food item gets its name from an Italian word meaning 'pie'?
    a) Biscuit
    b) Croissant
    c) Pizza
    d) Cake

WEEK 2

1. According to the 2011 census, which Indian state has the lowest population density?
2. What are Robusta, Rasthali, Poovan, Singapuri and Chinia types of?
3. The British prime minister in 1830–34 gives his name to which variety of tea?
4. Who was the first woman to win the Dadasaheb Phalke Award?
5. The Durand Line separates Pakistan and which other country?
6. Which famous battle took place in Bengal on 23 June 1757?
7. Which famous brand of toothpaste was introduced in a collapsible tube in 1896?
8. Which novel by Ruskin Bond was made into the film *Junoon*, by Shyam Benegal?

9. Which national park in India has the largest population of Asiatic Lions?
10. Which former football manager coined the phrase 'squeaky-bum time' to refer to the tense final stages of a league competition?
11. Which river has the largest drainage system in the world in terms of the volume of its flow and the area of its basin?
    a) Nile
    b) Amazon
    c) Brahmaputra
    d) Danube
12. Which of these shares its name with an island off the west coast of Italy?
    a) Capri
    b) Cardigan
    c) Wellington
    d) Palazzo

WEEK 3

1. In which town is the cattle fair called Harihar Kshetra Mela held every year?
2. Of all the states in northeast India, which is the largest state in terms of area?
3. Of all the members of the United Nations (UN) with names starting with the letter N, how many are in Africa?
4. Who was the first deputy prime minister of independent India?
5. Who played the role of Anwar Ali Anwar in the 1969 film *Saat Hindustani*?
6. Hachiro-gata is the lowest point of which country?
7. The archaeological ruins at Mohenjodaro, a UNESCO World Heritage Site, are located in which country?
8. Name the first Indian to win the 'Ernst & Young World Entrepreneur of the Year' award.
9. The Remington Model 1 that hit the shelves in 1873 was the first commercial variety of which machine?

10. The men's singles winner of which Grand Slam tournament is presented with the Norman Brookes Challenge Cup?

11. Which of these words means an exact copy, especially of written or printed material?

    a) Facsimile
    b) Halftone
    c) Hologram
    d) Blueprint

12. Who was the author of the epic poem *The Divine Comedy*?

    a) William Shakespeare
    b) Geoffrey Chaucer
    c) Walt Whitman
    d) Dante Alighieri

WEEK 4

1. According to Hindu legend, which city in Karnataka gets its name from Mahishasura, a mighty demon?
2. What is 'Triskaidekaphobia' the fear of?
3. Who was appointed the prime minister of Sri Lanka on 21 July 1960?
4. Which satirical British sitcom, written by Antony Jay and Jonathan Lynn, was first transmitted by the BBC between 1980 and 1984?
5. Which mountain peak was known as Peak XV before 1865?
6. In 1963, General Robert F. Kennedy authorized the FBI to tap the telephone of which leader?
7. The name of which national airline means 'union' in Arabic?
8. Which novel by Vikram Seth has 1,349 pages, 591,552 words and is one of the longest novels ever published?
9. Which of Einstein's possessions was divided into 240

blocks and distributed to researchers after his death in 1955?

10. The Oriental Circle in Bengaluru has been renamed after which Indian cricketer?

11. In 2007, the Nobel Peace Prize was awarded jointly to the Intergovernmental Panel on Climate Change (IPCC) and …

    a) Al Gore
    b) Joe Biden
    c) Wangari Maathai
    d) Erin Brockovich

12. Traditionally, the colours on a Margherita pizza is said to reflect the colours on the national flag of which of these countries?

    a) USA
    b) South Africa
    c) China
    d) Italy

WEEK 5

1. The proceedings of the Supreme Court of India are conducted in which language?
2. What connects the Bahai temple in Delhi, Nadroo Kebab, Rajiv Gandhi and *Nelumbo nucifera* (Gaertn)?
3. What is the election symbol of the Janata Dal (U)?
4. For which 1982 film did Richard Attenborough win the Academy Award for Best Director?
5. In which country is the famous Tribhuvan International Airport located?
6. The name of which fort in India comes from the Telugu words meaning 'Shepherd's Hill'?
7. In 1985, who became the founding President of the American Association of Ayurvedic Medicine?
8. Whose autobiography is titled *A Shot at History: My Obsessive Journey to Olympic Gold*?
9. The first indigenously built satellite of India was named after which astronomer?

10. How many overs a side were played in a match in the first World Cup in 1975?
11. In 1861, who patented an independently controlled steam engine for elevator use?
    a) Elisha Otis
    b) Nikola Tesla
    c) Cyrus Hall McCormick
    d) Samuel Colt
12. The goliath bird-eater tarantula is the world's largest …
    a) Butterfly
    b) Spider
    c) Earthworm
    d) Beetle

WEEK 6

1. Vidyadhar Bhattacharya was the chief architect and planner of which city in Rajasthan?
2. What has the Central Jail in Buxar been the official supplier of, for over a decade?
3. Which bird appears on the flag of Egypt?
4. Who was the first education minister of independent India?
5. In the 1970s, after which leader was Saigon renamed?
6. In the 1890s, whose visit to the US was funded by his disciples and the Raja of Khetri?
7. In the public sector undertakings (PSUs), what can be offered by the Gujarat or DHI pattern?
8. Which Muslim scholar is the author of *Kitab fi Tahqiq ma li'l-Hind*?
9. Which breed of dog is sometimes called the 'barkless dog'?
10. What kind of animal was Fuleco, the official mascot of the 2014 FIFA World Cup?

11. Which of these video games is based on a series by Terry Pratchett?
    a) Stuntman
    b) Discworld
    c) Super Hexagon
    d) Berzerk
12. Which spice is called *Acafrao-da-India* in Portuguese?
    a) Saffron
    b) Cinnamon
    c) Fennel
    d) Turmeric

WEEK 7

1. In which state were the first Aadhar cards issued?
2. According to legend, Kashmiri shawls reached Europe after which emperor presented one to his wife?
3. In Roman numerals, which letter is used to denote 100?
4. Who is the famous mother of the gentlemen, Tej Pratap and Tejaswi?
5. Which film consists of four short films: *Ajeeb Dastan Hai Yeh*, *Star*, *Sheela Ki Jawani* and *Murabba*?
6. In which state of India is the Surajkund International Crafts Mela held?
7. Name the India club which won the first National Football League.
8. Whose diary was saved by her family's helper, Miep Gies, and first published in 1947?
9. Which is the largest joint in the human body?
10. In which state is Sivakasi, a town that accounts for 90 per cent of firecracker production in the country, located?

11. A large Maasai warrior's shield covering crossed spears is superimposed at the center of the national flag of which country?
    a) Kenya
    b) North Korea
    c) Chile
    d) Oman
12. The name of which animal means 'earth pig' in the Afrikaans language?
    a) Aardvark
    b) Sloth
    c) Tapir
    d) Pangolin

WEEK 8

1. In India, National Science Day is celebrated on 28 February every year to commemorate the discovery of what?
2. The Bandra–Worli Sea Link is officially named after which former prime minister?
3. What connects Michael Phelps, a spider and the Zodiac sign Scorpio?
4. In 1964, which finance minister presented the annual budget of India on his birthday, 29 February?
5. Who composed the music for Richard Attenborough's *Gandhi*?
6. The eruptions of the Krakatoa and El Chichon volcanoes in 1883 and 1983 respectively led to which now-popular phenomenon?
7. Which is the world's most expensive spice by weight?
8. According to Mark Twain, which city is 'older than history, older than tradition, older even than legend'?

9. Io, Europa, Ganymede and Callisto are the moons of which planet?
10. In 1903, which sporting event was started by the editor of *L' Auto* to increase the circulation of the newspaper?
11. Which of these sarees is named after a district in Odisha?
    a) Chanderi
    b) Pochampally
    c) Kanjeevaram
    d) Sambalpuri
12. If Hellenic Republic is the long form of the name of this country, what is its conventional short form?
    a) Greece
    b) France
    c) Austria
    d) Italy

WEEK 9

1. Ranjana Sonawane is the first Indian to receive what?
2. Nawab Wajid Ali Shah added which vegetable to the Awadhi biryani?
3. Which creature appears on the logo of the World Health Organization?
4. Which Indian politician's father coined the term 'Lokpal' in the early 1960s?
5. Who was the first choice for the role of Gabbar Singh in the 1975 film *Sholay*?
6. In which northeastern state in India is the world's only floating national park, Keibul Lamjao, located?
7. According to legend, the name of which island country was given by Sang Nila Utama, the ruler of Palembang?
8. Which is the first book in the Ibis trilogy by Amitav Ghosh?
9. Who became the first American in space on 5 May 1961?
10. Who is the first-ever India-born winner of the PGA Tour?

11. Using a smartphone to connect a computer or other device to the Internet, is called ...
    a) Tethering
    b) Buffering
    c) Booting
    d) Scrolling
12. Which singer was rechristened after a famous character from her father's play 'Bhaaw Bandhan'?
    a) Asha Bhosle
    b) Lata Mangeshkar
    c) Kavita Krishnamurthy
    d) Shreya Ghoshal

WEEK 10

1. MARCOS is an elite operations unit of which arm of the Indian Armed Forces?
2. Kollywood is the film industry of which Indian state?
3. Between 1885 and 1916, a series of lavish Easter eggs were created by Fabergé for the Imperial family of which country?
4. Who is the only US President to serve two non-consecutive terms?
5. How is the performer Armando Christian Pérez better known?
6. Which famous temple is situated on Neelachal Parbat or Kamagiri in the city of Guwahati?
7. With a height of 72.5 metres, which UNESCO World Heritage site is the highest stone tower in India?
8. Which ad guru wrote the tagline 'The Tyre with Muscle' for MRF?

9. Cartoonist R.K. Laxman specialized in painting which birds?
10. In 1610, which astronomer was the first to gaze at Saturn through a telescope?
11. Which scientist published *An Essay on the Shaking Palsy* in 1817?
    a) Christiaan Barnard
    b) Edward Jenner
    c) James Parkinson
    d) William Harvey
12. Which of these instruments does not have keys on it?
    a) Accordion
    b) Piano
    c) Banjo
    d) Synthesizer

WEEK 11

1. On the eve of which national holiday are the Padma Awards announced?
2. Which flower connects hybrid tea, Kate Winslet in *Titanic* and a novel by Italian author Umberto Eco?
3. In 1969, which post did Shyam Nandan Mishra first occupy in the Rajya Sabha?
4. Satyajit Ray described which Bollywood actor, born in 1922, as 'the ultimate method actor'?
5. Pidurutalagala is the highest point of which country?
6. Which poet from the court of Raja Laxman Sen of Bengal wrote *Geet Govinda*?
7. Which famous Indian brand is named after Ramniklal Ambani's son?
8. In which comic strip, known for its satirical office humour, are you most likely to meet a character named Asok?
9. On which planet would you find a high plateau named Lakshmi Planum?

10. The first name of which Indian footballer means 'little brother' in Tibetan?
11. In DNS, if 'N' stands for 'Name' and 'S' stands for 'System', what does 'D' stand for?
    a) Draft
    b) Dashboard
    c) Digital
    d) Domain
12. Red cost, Premier and Pusa Early Dwarf are varieties of which fruit?
    a) Apple
    b) Pomegranate
    c) Litchi
    d) Strawberry

WEEK 12

1. Which item of India's national pride was based upon a design by Pingali Venkayya?
2. What name did the Delhi Special Establishment Police get through the Home Ministry Resolution of 1 April 1963?
3. Which country immediately follows India in the alphabetical list of member countries of the UN?
4. In India, a person holding which position is also the ex-officio Chairman of the Rajya Sabha?
5. In which film, starring Aamir Khan, did Nawazuddin Siddiqui make his debut?
6. In which city is the seat of the International Court of Justice located?
7. Which emperor's greatest victory was at the Battle of Gaugamela?
8. Along with Gary Hamel, who created the original concept of 'core competencies'?

9. Which scientist was appointed Warden of the British Royal Mint in 1696?
10. The Indian cricket team plays against which team for the Pataudi Trophy?
11. Alfred Nobel coined the word 'dynamite' from a Greek word meaning …
    a) Cracker
    b) Burst
    c) Power
    d) Gun powder
12. After which author's work is the Godan Express named?
    a) Valmiki
    b) Munshi Premchand
    c) Kalidasa
    d) Bhisham Sahni

WEEK 13

1. Which famous train was introduced in India on 1 March 1969?
2. In which month does the financial year of India start?
3. Which was the first organization to receive three Nobel Peace Prizes?
4. In 1964, who was named Minister of Information and Broadcasting in Lal Bahadur Shastri's government?
5. Who sang the song 'Teri Mehfil Mein Qismat' along with Shamshad Begum, in *Mughal-E-Azam*?
6. On which river is the Nagarjuna Sagar Dam built?
7. If you were visiting the site of the First Battle of Panipat (fought on 21 April 1526), which state would you be in?
8. Which is the first alcoholic beverage from India to get the GI status?
9. On the outskirts of which city is the headquarters of World Health Organization located?
10. In which sport did Leander Paes' mother represent India

at the 1972 Summer Olympics Games?

11. Bagru, Sanganer and Barmeri are printing techniques unique to which state of India?
    a) Kerala
    b) Maharashtra
    c) Rajasthan
    d) Bihar
12. The white colour on the flag of Chile represents the snow-covered ...
    a) Rockies
    b) Andes
    c) Alps
    d) Himalayas

WEEK 14

1. Which Indian city was the first to introduce CNG-electric hybrid buses?
2. What connects C. Rajagopalachari, Adi Kavi and Shatrughan Sinha?
3. The branches of which tree symbolise peace on the UN flag?
4. Which heroine was reading an Alistar MacLean thriller on a train, while the hero sang 'Mere Sapnon Ki Rani' in the film *Aradhana*?
5. Which waterway is called 'Qanat as-Suways' in Arabic?
6. If Qutb-ud-Din Aibak built the first storey of the Qutb Minar, who added three more storeys to it?
7. In 1970, the National Dairy Development Board initiated which operation to increase the availability of milk?
8. What breed of dog is Tintin's companion Snowy?
9. After which astronaut was the first dedicated meteorological satellite of India named?

10. Who was nicknamed 'Payyoli Express'?

11. Part II of the Constitution of India deals with ...

    a) Fundamental Rights
    b) The Union and its Territory
    c) Citizenship
    d) The States

12. Which of these words comes from the Latin word meaning 'hair'?

    a) Canal
    b) Artery
    c) Vein
    d) Capillary

WEEK 15

1. There are three national holidays in India: 26 January, 15 August and...
2. Who is the first Indian Nobel Prize winner to not win the Bharat Ratna?
3. In India, who was the first prime minister to sign a banknote?
4. Who directed the 1997 film *Chachi 420*?
5. The name of which hill-station in India comes from the Tibetan words meaning 'thunderbolt' and 'land'?
6. Which freedom fighter compiled the *Gita Rahasya*, a treatise on the *Bhagavad Gita*, during his stay in Burma (Myanmar)?
7. Retail business: Expand the abbreviation BOGOF.
8. What road did Rudyard Kipling describe as the 'backbone of all Hind'?
9. Whose official Twitter account sent out its first tweet 'HABEMUS PAPAM FRANCISCUM'?

10. On Sachin Tendulkar's Test debut, who took his wicket?

11. The word petroleum comes from the Latin words 'petra' and 'oleum'. If 'oleum' means oil, then 'petra' means…

    a) Fire
    b) Gas
    c) Ocean
    d) Rock

12. In 1933, who appointed Joseph Goebbels to the post of the minister for public enlightenment and propaganda?

    a) Adolf Hitler
    b) Benito Mussolini
    c) Joseph Stalin
    d) Mao Zedong

WEEK 16

1. The name of which Indian state, formed in 2000, means 'land with forest cover'?
2. Normally, what happens to the wood of the new rath after the Rath Yatra in Puri is over?
3. What connects Charlie Chaplin, California and pyrite?
4. Against which prime minister was the first no-confidence motion in the Lok Sabha moved by socialist Acharya Kripalani?
5. Who played the role of Abhimanyu Rai in the TV series *Fauji*?
6. In 2008, which river was declared the National River of India?
7. The mascot of which mobile app is named 'Ghostface Chillah'?
8. Whose autobiography is titled *Toward Freedom*?
9. Which is the smallest recognized breed of dog?

10. The Olympic flag features a blue ring, a yellow ring, a green ring, a black ring and a____
11. In QR code, if Q stands for 'quick', what does R stand for?
    a) Routing
    b) Registry
    c) Ranging
    d) Response
12. The Jurassic Period is named after a ...
    a) Mountain range
    b) River
    c) Town in France
    d) Reptile

WEEK 17

1. Apart from Madhya Pradesh, Uttarakhand and Uttar Pradesh, in which other state is the Kumbh Mela held?
2. If you were writing the names of the states of India in English, which would be the only state not to have an 'a' in its name?
3. According to popular belief, Francesco del Giocondo's wife is the subject of which famous painting?
4. Who was elected to the Maharashtra Legislative Assembly from the Latur constituency in 1980?
5. Which Bollywood film tells the story of a police inspector of Lalgunj, Uttar Pradesh?
6. Which state in northeastern India harbours the maximum number of orchid species in the country?
7. What had Mahatma Gandhi not seen till 1908 when he described it in *Hind Swaraj*?
8. In India, the Kimberley Process Certification Scheme certifies which valuable mineral?

9. Who wrote the book *Train to Pakistan*?
10. Architect Herbert Baker presented the weathervane named 'Father Time' to which iconic cricket ground?
11. The first stanza of which poem, published in *Tattvabodhini Patrika* in 1911, became the national anthem of India?
    a) *Vande Mataram*
    b) *Matribhumi*
    c) *Bharat Vidhata*
    d) *To Freedom*
12. In 1916, which leader defended Bal Gangadhar Tilak in his trial and became his partner in the signing of the Lucknow Pact?
    a) Jawaharlal Nehru
    b) Mahatma Gandhi
    c) Chittaranjan Das
    d) Muhammed Ali Jinnah

WEEK 18

1. Which classical dance form shares its name with a village in the Divi taluka of Krishna district in Andhra Pradesh?
2. Which American architect designed the Indian Institute of Management (IIM) campus in Ahmedabad?
3. Hamid Ansari is the second Vice-President of India to get a second consecutive term. Who was the first?
4. In 2009, the makers of which Oscar-winning film donated 500,000 pounds towards child development in Mumbai?
5. The name of which mountain peak means 'Five Treasures of the Eternal Snow' in Tibetan?
6. Who was the first Mughal emperor to be born in present-day India?
7. Which variety of mango was used to make Frooti when it was launched?
8. Before Eleanor Catton, who was the youngest woman to win the Man Booker Prize?

9. Who discovered the presence of the malarial parasite within the female Anopheles mosquito in 1897?
10. With which sport is the Calcutta Cup, played between England and Scotland, associated?
11. What is a machine, used to change liquid medication into vapour so that it can be inhaled, called?
    a) Conciser
    b) Dialyser
    c) Analyser
    d) Nebuliser
12. Who travelled in the van, 'Mystery Machine', with four young friends?
    a) Mickey Mouse
    b) Bugs Bunny
    c) Scooby Doo
    d) Garfield

WEEK 19

1. Which tourist attraction in Chandigarh was created by Nek Chand?
2. In 1981, who did the Israel Philharmonic Orchestra award the title, Music Director for Life?
3. Which Indian leader received the Best Parliamentarian Award in 1997?
4. Murphy Radio claimed that their trademark Murphy baby was used in which 2012 Bollywood film?
5. K2, the second highest peak in the world, is situated in which mountain range?
6. The Mughal Emperor Babur valued what as 'two-and-a-half days' food of the entire world'?
7. Who is the originator of 'lateral thinking'?
8. How do we know the author Charles Lutwidge Dodgson better?
9. Hotmail was founded by Jack Smith and …?

10. Off whose bowling did Yuvraj Singh hit six sixes in an over in the 2007 ICC World Twenty20 championship?

11. Laser, inkjet and thermal are different types of ...

    a) Monitors
    b) Digital cameras
    c) Computer printers
    d) Mouse

12. Which dog is named after a Norwegian term of affection?

    a) Snowy
    b) Snoopy
    c) Pluto
    d) Goofy

WEEK 20

1. Which supersonic cruise missile is named after the Brahmaputra and Moskva rivers?
2. Totapuri, Amrapalli and Fazli are different varieties of which fruit?
3. Which African city took its name from a water hole which translates to 'Cold Water'?
4. Who was the first President of India to live in the Rashtrapati Bhawan?
5. How is the actress Shree Amma Yanger more popularly known?
6. If you were visiting the Group of Monuments at Hampi, which Indian state would you be in?
7. In 1604, Baba Buddha was appointed as the first keeper of which religious book?
8. Who created the mascot called Gattu, once used by Asian Paints?

9. Which fictional town is located on the banks of the Sarayu river?
10. Which was the first Indian club to represent the country in the finals of the Asian Cup Championship in 1985–86?
11. Which of these is the angriest bird in the 'Angry Bird' series?
    a) Red
    b) Blue
    c) Yellow
    d) Green
12. Which singer was born as Hirdesh Singh?
    a) Mika Singh
    b) Himesh Reshammiya
    c) Honey Singh
    d) Hard Kaur

WEEK 21

1. Which Special Response Unit uses the Sudarshan Chakra as its logo?
2. What connects the Brahmaputra, Godan, Azad Hind, Kumbh and Padmavati?
3. According to a survey of Global Business Schools by *The Economist* in 2009, which management institute is the 'toughest in the world to get into'?
4. In 2012, Francois Hollande became the President of which country?
5. In 2003, who became the first Indian actor to be a member of the jury at the Cannes Film Festival?
6. In 1947, the Radcliffe Line became the border between India and which country?
7. Which monument, originally made in wood, represented the saint Imam Hussain's tomb?
8. Which famous Indian brand was named after Nirupama Patel?

9. What is Donald Duck's middle name?
10. The last digit of the Play Station model number denotes where it is sold. If 1 is US, what is 0?
11. Who became the head of the radiological service of the International Red Cross during World War I?
    a) Rosalind Franklin
    b) Edward Jenner
    c) Marie Curie
    d) Louis Pasteur
12. Which of these is a rich fruit cake, typically decorated on top with almonds?
    a) Paella
    b) Ratatouille
    c) Dundee
    d) Lasagne

WEEK 22

1. The Parliament Library, Delhi is India's second largest library. Which city houses India's largest library?
2. Gyaldun Dasho Thinley Dorji wrote the lyrics of the national anthem of which country?
3. Which President of India also served as the Indian High Commissioner in Ceylon (Sri Lanka) between 1947 and 1951?
4. In Telugu, it is *Vikramarkudu*. In Tamil, it is *Siruthai*. Which Bollywood film am I talking about?
5. In which Indian state is the industrial town, Vasco da Gama, located?
6. In 326 BC, which Indian ruler presented 30 pounds of Indian iron to Alexander?
7. Name the ad guru who sold pressure cookers and worked as a chef before starting his agency.
8. *Life on the Mississippi* is a memoir by which famous author?
9. Dhoom.com is the website of which Indian band?

10. Till 2015, who had scored the most number of runs in the IPL?

11. Which of these is an optical instrument that is used for the visual examination of the abdominal cavity?

    a) Polariscope
    b) Oscilloscope
    c) Laparoscope
    d) Statoscope

12. Devi Ahilya Bai Holkar Airport serves which city of India?

    a) Jabalpur
    b) Indore
    c) Gwalior
    d) Bhopal

WEEK 23

1. By what name do we popularly know the town of Sohra in Meghalaya?
2. Which sitarist was awarded India's highest civilian honour, the Bharat Ratna, in 1999?
3. Whose autobiography is titled *Long Walk to Freedom*?
4. Barack Obama's father was a senior governmental economist of which country?
5. Who won the Filmfare Award for Best Actor for the film *Sachaa Jhutha*?
6. The melting water of which glacier is the main source of water for the Nubra river?
7. What was the name of the first planned city of the Mughals?
8. Which two-word phrase did writer Suketu Mehta coin to describe Mumbai?
9. The name of which fish means 'tooth fish' in the Tupi language?

10. At Lord's, who was the first Indian to score a century on his Test debut?
11. In 1818, what was first successfully performed by James Blundell?
    a) Human blood transfusion
    b) Cornea transplant
    c) Caesarian section
    d) Skin grafting
12. Mount Rushmore shows the carved heads of George Washington, Thomas Jefferson, Theodore Roosevelt and …
    a) Richard Nixon
    b) Gerald Ford
    c) Woodrow Wilson
    d) Abraham Lincoln

WEEK 24

1. Sardar Vallabhbhai Patel International Airport serves which Indian city?
2. The 2011 film *The King's Speech* is based on the life of which English king?
3. Which Indian prime minister never faced Parliament, even though he was in office for 171 days?
4. In which Indian state would you be served a 36-course meal called Wazwan?
5. With which country does India share its longest international boundary?
6. In 1979, the Nobel banquet in Oslo was cancelled on whose request?
7. Which Indian economist coined the phrase 'Hindu rate of growth'?
8. Forest Officer Gisborne offered which fictional character a job as a Forest Ranger?

9. ________was the text of the first SMS sent by Neil Papworth in 1992. Fill in the blanks.

10. In 1958, who became the first Indian male to win a gold medal in athletics at the Commonwealth Games?

11. In 2012, which of these was named as the most important invention in the history of food by the Royal Society of UK?

    a) Refrigerator
    b) Microwave oven
    c) Mixer
    d) Knife

12. At the Academy Awards, which Indian film lost to *Nights in Cabiria* by one vote?

    a) *Lagaan*
    b) *Mother India*
    c) *Mughal-e-Azam*
    d) *Salaam Bombay*

WEEK 25

1. Whose debut album was titled *Come Away with Me*?
2. Which board game was originally called 'Mokshapat'?
3. The verses of the national anthem of which country were composed by Abul Asar Hafeez Jullundhri?
4. Who wrote the book entitled *Painting as a Pastime*?
5. Which director did actress Kalki Koechlin marry on 30 April 2011?
6. Which river has the largest river basin in India?
7. Which famous salutation is said to have been coined by Chempakaraman Pillai during the independence movement?
8. Ashok Leyland is the flagship company of which group?
9. Which snake is called 'matatoro' or 'bull killer' by the Spanish?
10. In 2010, against which team did Sachin Tendulkar hit the first ODI double century?

11. Which of these words comes from the French word meaning 'to hide'?

    a) Captcha
    b) Dashboard
    c) Cookie
    d) Cache

12. *Sayaun Thunga Phool Ka* or *Hundreds of Flowers* is the national anthem of which country?

    a) China
    b) Sri Lanka
    c) Nepal
    d) Japan

WEEK 26

1. Apart from Assam and Manipur, with which Indian state does Mizoram share its border?
2. In whose honour does India celebrate 22 December as 'National Mathematics Day'?
3. In 1953, Winston Churchill received the Nobel Prize in which category?
4. Who was the first UN Secretary-General to be elected from the ranks of UN staff?
5. Who played the role of Dr Rajit Ratha in the film *The Amazing Spider-Man*?
6. The real name of which Indian ruler was Budh Singh?
7. Who was the founding editor of *Stardust* and *Celebrity*?
8. In the Harry Potter books, who is the twin sister of Parvati Patil?
9. In 1905, on visiting which national park did Lady Curzon persuade her husband to save the rhinos?

10. The late Wilson Jones from India was a world champion in which sport?
11. In 2011, what did Mark Zuckerberg introduce as 'all your stories, all your apps and a new way to express who you are.'?
    a) Scrapbook
    b) Wall
    c) Timeline
    d) Cover
12. Who translated Mahatma Gandhi's *The Story of My Experiments with Truth* into English?
    a) Jawaharlal Nehru
    b) R. K. Narayan
    c) Sarojini Naidu
    d) Mahadev Desai

WEEK 27

1. Whose autobiography is titled *Pandharpur Ka Ek Ladka*?
2. The scientific name of which tree is *Azadirachta indica* meaning the 'Free Tree of India'?
3. What connects a play by G.B. Shaw, a record label founded by The Beatles in 1968 and Golden Delicious?
4. In 1971, which cricketer contested the Lok Sabha elections from Gurgaon as a nominee of the Vishal Haryana Party?
5. With which film did Aamir Khan make his directorial debut?
6. What is the name of India's highest waterfall?
7. In 1591, which monument was built by Mohammed Quli Qutab Shah to commemorate the end of the plague in Hyderabad?
8. Where in India did Facebook open its first office?
9. In 1992, who received the Sahitya Akademi Award for *Our Trees Still Grow in Dehra*?

10. Which breed of dog is the fictional character, Scooby-Doo?
11. What name, meaning 'Bringer of Light', was adopted by Nguyen That Thanh?
    a) Che Guevara
    b) Fidel Castro
    c) Ho Chi Minh
    d) Adolf Hitler
12. Which of these incidents occurred for the first time in 1984?
    a) India got its first female Prime Minister
    b) An Indian woman summitted Mount Everest
    c) India won an Olympic gold
    d) Tiger census was conducted

WEEK 28

1. What is the common name of the Hindu festival Dhulheti or Phagwa?
2. In 1950, who established the Missionaries of Charity in Calcutta?
3. The Fisherman's Ring is the signet ring of a person holding which position?
4. Who served as the Deputy Chairperson of the Rajya Sabha from 1986 to 1988?
5. The film cans for the advance screening of which 1997 film had the code name 'Baby's Day Out 2'?
6. The statue of Mahishasura on the Chamundi Hills is a major attraction of which Indian state?
7. Which historical figure was born as Farid Khan?
8. In 1967, which entrepreneur joined the travel business as a GSA for the Lebanese International Airlines?
9. Which fictional character married an Indian princess named Aouda?

10. Which famous football club is run by the Alemao family of Goa?
11. Which famous painter painted the *Battle of Anghiari*?
    a) Pablo Picasso
    b) Leonardo da Vinci
    c) Rembrandt
    d) Raphael
12. Russian Caravan and Lapsang Souchong are varieties of ...
    a) Orange
    b) Tea
    c) Apple
    d) Coffee

WEEK 29

1. Lachchu Maharaj was an exponent of which dance form?
2. Which Beatle named his son Dhani, after two notes of the Indian music scale?
3. Which was the first country in the world to have a complete set of banknotes made from polymer?
4. In 1971, which economist joined the Government of India as Economic Advisor in the commerce ministry?
5. Whose autobiography is titled *Romancing with Life*?
6. In which UNESCO World Heritage site would you find the famous Quwwat ul-Islam Mosque?
7. Which Mughal emperor founded a religious doctrine called Din-i-Ilahi?
8. Which six-letter word that originated from French and means a social event at which each guest contributes a share of the food?
9. Name the only state where the Sangai deer exists in its natural habitat.

10. India-born Narottam 'Tom' Puna played Test cricket for which country?
11. To whom did Tracy Chapman dedicate her song 'Freedom Now'?
    a) Mahatma Gandhi
    b) Nelson Mandela
    c) Mother Teresa
    d) Dalai Lama
12. Which of these organs regulates blood volume and destroys old red blood cells?
    a) Gallbladder
    b) Pancreas
    c) Heart
    d) Liver

WEEK 30

1. Which percussionist founded Moment Records in 1991?
2. According to Hindu mythology Sri Krishna died on the first day of which yug?
3. Who served as the Principal Scientific Advisor to the Government of India from November 1999 to November 2001?
4. How is Dhundiraj Govind Phalke better known to us?
5. Which five-storey building has 953 pink sandstone windows known as 'jharokhas'?
6. Which was the earliest authoritative text on public finance, administration and fiscal laws in India?
7. Which ad agency created the Zoozoo characters for Vodafone?
8. Which comic-strip character is known as Iron Arm in Italy and Karl Alfred in Sweden?
9. In which state of India is the Indian Wild Ass Sanctuary situated?

10. Which Rajiv Gandhi Khel Ratna awardee made his Hindi film debut with *Rajdhani Express*?
11. In 1846, which planet was first observed by the German astronomer, Johann Gottfried Galle?
    a) Jupiter
    b) Mars
    c) Neptune
    d) Saturn
12. In 2013, who became the youngest English player to score a century in the Ashes?
    a) Alastair Cook
    b) Joe Root
    c) Ben Stokes
    d) Jos Buttler

WEEK 31

1. Who, among the Beatles, bought a sitar to record the song 'Norwegian Wood'?
2. Who was the first Asian to head an Oxbridge college?
3. Who is the National Poet of Pakistan?
4. Which Hindi film actor made his directorial debut with the 1974 film *Manoranjan*?
5. Midan Ismailiya in Cairo, Egypt is now popularly known by what name?
6. Which famous Indian building was built using 700 million bricks and three million cubic feet of stone?
7. Rugmark is the international label against illegal child labour in the ____ industry. Fill in the blank.
8. Who created the character called 'The Common Man'?
9. The fish Bombil is also known as ____ Duck. Fill in the blank.
10. Till 2014, who was the only cricketer to have won more than 20 Man-of-the-Match awards in Test cricket?

11. On February 12, 1948, whose ashes were carried to Triveni in a third class compartment numbered 2949?
    a) Mahatma Gandhi
    b) Lal Bahadur Shastri
    c) Jawaharlal Nehru
    d) Bal Gangadhar Tilak
12. At an entrance to which cave would you find the masterpiece *Sadashiva*?
    a) Ajanta Caves
    b) Ellora Caves
    c) Borra Caves
    d) Elephanta Caves

WEEK 32

1. In India, which was the first government organisation to join Twitter?
2. Which is the only Indian monument to appear on the list of the New Seven Wonders of the World?
3. In which country is the famous Temple of Preah Vihear, a UNESCO World Heritage Site, located?
4. Who was the first non-Indian head of state to receive India's highest civilian award, the Bharat Ratna?
5. Which artist directed a short film called *Through the Eyes of a Painter* in 1967?
6. Located in Bijapur, what is the name of the mausoleum of Muhammad Adil Shah?
7. In 1493, which explorer wrote a report on his discoveries of the 'Islands of India beyond the Ganges'?
8. Who was the first non-European to win the Nobel Prize for Literature?

9. Which national park is home to more than 86 per cent of the total population of rhinoceroses in India?
10. In 2012, Roger Federer equalled whose record as the No. 1 men's player for a total of 285 weeks?
11. The Chipko movement, which began in 1973, was associated with ...
    a) Gender equality
    b) Forest conservation
    c) Safety for miners
    d) Sanitation
12. A character created by Jules Verne, also known as Prince Dakkar, was the nephew of which Indian king?
    a) Prithviraj Chauhan
    b) Akbar
    c) Chhatrapati Shivaji
    d) Tipu Sultan

WEEK 33

1. On the National Emblem of India, which animal is the guardian of the east?
2. Which fruit are Anab-e-Shahi, Bangalore Blue and Sharad Seedless varieties of?
3. Which country was referred to as 'Serendib' by the Arabs?
4. Who has been the only woman finance minister of India?
5. Who won the first Filmfare Award for Best Actor?
6. Which gateway in Lucknow was modelled after the Sublime Porte in Istanbul?
7. Which ruler looted the Peacock Throne in 1739?
8. In 1965, which company pioneered Son-et-lumiere shows at the Red Fort?
9. Which author went to watch a magic show by Mr Electrico and heard the words 'Live forever!' directed at him?
10. Till 2015, which West-Indian jointly held the record of scoring the fastest century in Test cricket, in terms of the number of balls?

11. The name of which flightless bird comes from the Polynesian word for fowl?

    a) Moa
    b) Ostrich
    c) Penguin
    d) Kiwi

12. What appears on the logo of the Ecomark scheme in India?

    a) A coconut shell
    b) A stalk of rice
    c) An earthen pot
    d) A banyan tree

WEEK 34

1. In 2004, the famous European Case Awards instituted an award for Excellence in Case Writing and named it after which Indian?
2. What became the tallest structure in the world in 1889?
3. Who appoints the Chief Election Commissioners and Election Commissioners in India?
4. Which film director is the founder of the film production company 'Mukta Arts Limited'?
5. The land for which UNESCO World Heritage site was acquired from the Kachhwahas of Ajmer in lieu of four havelis?
6. In 2003, what 'piece' of Indian history was bought by an Indian at an auction in England?
7. Which building would you see on the reverse side of a Rs 50 note?
8. Which eight-letter word in English comes from the Latin word meaning 'entity or concern of the people'?

9. With which creature is the wildlife conservationist Romulus Whitaker synonymous?
10. Which is the oldest Test cricket venue in England?
11. In 1985, a group of scientists published the first paper on springtime losses of ozone over which region?
    a) North Pole
    b) Mariana Trench
    c) Antarctica
    d) Mount Everest
12. In 1940, who became the first African-American woman to win an Oscar?
    a) Pam Grier
    b) Nichelle Nichols
    c) Hattie McDaniel
    d) Dorothy Dandridge

WEEK 35

1. Who designed the uniforms of the Goa Traffic Police?
2. Dal-baati-churma is a famous dish of which Indian state?
3. What connects Morris Michtom, Mr Bean and Stratford-upon-Avon?
4. India is a part of the Commonwealth. Who is the Head of the Commonwealth?
5. Screenwriter Simon Beaufoy visited India while writing the screenplay of which film?
6. After the Taj Mahal, which was the most visited monument in India in 2009?
7. Which Indian emperor wrote the three Sanskrit plays, *Nagananda*, *Ratnavali* and *Priyadarsika*?
8. Which comic strip character has a Dollarmation dog named Dollar?
9. According to data compiled in 2014, which Asian country had the most number of Internet users?

10. Who is the first Indian player to play for the Major League Soccer club, Kansas City Wizards?

11. The Mantoux test is done to find out if you have come in contact with the bacteria that causes ...

    a) Osteomyelitis
    b) Tuberculosis
    c) Diptheria
    d) Tetanus

12. Who received the Nobel Prize 'for his part in the invention of the integrated circuit'?

    a) Jack Kilby
    b) Walter Brattain
    c) Jerry Yang
    d) Dorothy Hodgkin

WEEK 36

1. In which Indian state is the tribal fair, Chitra-Vichitra Mela held?
2. The headquarters of SAARC are located in which neighbouring country of India?
3. In India, who is the first person to be enumerated in the census?
4. Who played the role of Batman in the 2012 film *The Dark Knight Rises*?
5. If you were visiting the Golden Temple of Dambulla, which country would you be in?
6. Which emperor defeated Rana Sanga at the Battle of Khanwa in 1527?
7. Mr WizeR is the mascot of which brand of cars?
8. *Going Solo* is a memoir by which famous author?
9. Hailey National Park was renamed after which hunter turned conservationist?

10. Till 2015, who has hit the most number of sixes in the ICC World Twenty20?

11. Who invented the 'Crescograph' to record plant growth?

    a) Satyendra Nath Bose
    b) Meghnad Saha
    c) Jagadish Chandra Bose
    d) Prafulla Chandra Ray

12. A red scroll on the national flag of Spain bears the motto 'Plus Ultra', which means ...

    a) Truly Beyond
    b) Further Beyond
    c) Freedom Beyond
    d) Nothing Beyond

WEEK 37

1. When the Indian government launched the e-passports scheme, who received the first copy?
2. 110201 is the new dedicated pin code of which important landmark in New Delhi?
3. Jackson Heights is the 'Little India' of which American city?
4. Under Article 76 of the Constitution, who appoints the Attorney General of India?
5. Which Bollywood actress won the Miss World title in 2000?
6. Which international airport in India has the International Civil Aviation Organization (ICAO) code VECC?
7. Ustad Ahmad and Ustad Hamid were the architects of which famous landmark in Delhi?
8. Who was infamously convicted in a case filed in 1995 by the solicitor firm, Poornanand and Company?

9. *The Fall of a Sparrow* is the autobiography of which famous Indian ornithologist?
10. St Leo is the middle name of Wellesley and Jennifer's famous son. Name him.
11. The first major optical telescope placed in space was named after whom?
    a) William Herschel
    b) Albert Einstein
    c) Isaac Newton
    d) Edwin Hubble
12. The Zika virus is named after a forest in which country?
    a) Uganda
    b) Somalia
    c) Tanzania
    d) Libya

WEEK 38

1. Who first gave the title 'Mahatma' to Mohandas Karamchand Gandhi?
2. Which state in India is famous for its Sambalpuri saris?
3. Who resigned as the chief minister of Karnataka to be sworn in as the eleventh prime minister of India?
4. The real name of which Bollywood actor is Rajiv Hari Om Bhatia?
5. In which country is the Borobudur temple located?
6. In 1937–38, the British government decided to repatriate the prisoners from this famous prison with 698 cells. Name it.
7. Which famous advertising icon was created by Eustace Fernandes?
8. In 1993, who was awarded the 'Booker of Bookers' Prize?
9. Which disease has been responsible for half of all human deaths since the Stone Age?

10. Among Indians, who has officiated as a match referee in the most number of ODI matches?
11. Galileo Galilei is said to have performed his experiment of gravity from which of these structures?
    a) Statue of Liberty
    b) Eiffel Tower
    c) Leaning Tower of Pisa
    d) Big Ben
12. On whose life is the Martin Scorsese-directed film *Kundun* based?
    a) Mahatma Gandhi
    b) Dalai Lama
    c) Nelson Mandela
    d) Mother Teresa

WEEK 39

1. In which capital city of India is the famous Ujjayanta Palace located?
2. ADI is the railway station code of which city?
3. The words ORDEM E PROGRESSO appear on the flag of which country?
4. Who appoints the Comptroller and Auditor-General of India?
5. The Salman Khan starrer film *Hello* is based on whose novel?
6. In about 1821, the name of which hill station first appeared in the *Madras Gazette* as 'Wotokymund'?
7. With which historical incident would you associate the three ships named Dartmouth, Eleanor and Beaver?
8. Dabur once marketed the drug Plagin to combat...
9. The word 'salary' comes from the Latin word salarium, originally denoting a Roman soldier's allowance to buy what?

10. During 1972–87, the Kooyong Lawn Tennis Club was the venue of which Grand Slam event?

11. What was the name of the first smartphone in the world?

    a) Luke
    b) William
    c) Simon
    d) Harvey

12. In 2015, which bird was voted the national bird of Great Britain?

    a) Robin
    b) Barn Owl
    c) Macaw
    d) Red kite

WEEK 40

1. The founders of Asian Paints derived the name of the company after randomly opening a…
2. Which Indian state was formed on 9 November 2000 as the 27th state of India?
3. Who received the Nobel Peace Prize in 2009?
4. Who is the only Speaker of the Lok Sabha to become the President of India?
5. Which actor, along with his wife, founded the production company 'Red Chillies Entertainment'?
6. According to a 2014 report, which city has the busiest airport in India in terms of passenger traffic?
7. *Rihla* is an account of whose travels?
8. What is the full form of the name of the charitable organization, CRY?
9. The extinct bird Moa was native to which country?
10. Till 2014, who, among Indians, has hit the most number of sixes in Test matches?

11. Cholecystitis is the acute or chronic inflammation of which organ?
    a) Eyes
    b) Gallbladder
    c) Lungs
    d) Appendix
12. Who paid a tribute to the film *The Sound of Music* on its 50th anniversary at the 2015 Academy Awards?
    a) Celine Dion
    b) Justin Bieber
    c) Lady Gaga
    d) Britney Spears

WEEK 41

1. In 1972, Jyoti Prasad Saikia, a journalist, coined which sobriquet for the Northeast?
2. Who was the first person outside the royal family, to appear on a British stamp?
3. Who was the first US president to visit India in his first term in office?
4. Which fictional character got his name from the French word for 'pool', specifically, a pool in which Francis Adirubasamy loved to swim?
5. On which Indian luxury train can you find two restaurant cars named Maharaja and Maharani?
6. In 1784, which monument was built by Nawab Asaf-ud-Daula in Lucknow in a famine relief programme?
7. Which airline in India has aircraft named Turmeric, Pepper and Cinnamon?
8. What was named 'Word of the Year for 2013' by the Oxford Dictionaries?

9. More than 600 places in Australia are named after which flightless bird?
10. After Raul left Real Madrid, who inherited his famous Number 7 shirt?
11. Who was trained at a young age by the KGB's infamous Red Room Academy?
    a) Black Widow
    b) Catwoman
    c) Storm
    d) Jean Grey
12. The World Malaria Report 2015 declared which of these as the first malaria-free region?
    a) Asia
    b) Africa
    c) Europe
    d) Australia

WEEK 42

1. Which is the second largest district of Maharashtra, in terms of area?
2. To visit the US, the people of which group require R-1 visas?
3. Daulatpur Nasirabad, a village in Haryana, was renamed in honour of which US President?
4. For which film did Lata Mangeshkar win the Rajat Kamal Award in 1991?
5. If you were visiting the Taj Mahal, in which Indian state would you be?
6. In 1854, the British offered an annual pension of Rs 60,000 to the widow of Raja Gangadhar Rao. Name her.
7. Harpal Singh of Delhi was the first proud Indian owner of which car?
8. In comics, which famous grandson of Will Fitzpatrick is a freelance photographer and science teacher?

9. Which achievement connects John Young, James Irwin, Alan Bean and a few others?
10. Who composed the official theme song of the 2010 Commonwealth Games?
11. Which of these cards would you come across in the game of Uno?
    a) Front Flip
    b) Wild Draw Four
    c) Show Your Card
    d) Pick 5
12. In 1982, which revolutionary object was named 'Machine of the Year' by *Time* magazine?
    a) Mobile phone
    b) Personal computer
    c) Digital camera
    d) Compact Disc

WEEK 43

1. Which religious leader introduced Mandala sand paintings?
2. In the 1840s, the first trial plantation of what was made by Dr A. Campbell?
3. The Daniel Guggenheim Medal was first conferred on Orville Wright. Who received it in 1988?
4. Shakti Sthal is the memorial of which Indian leader?
5. The name of which 2011 film is inspired from a song from the 1975 Dharmendra starrer *Pratiggya*?
6. Khajuraho is 25 km from the 'Mandla' gate of which tiger reserve?
7. Name the most famous son of Vishwanath Datta and Bhuvaneshwari Devi.
8. Which company started bhashaindia.com to promote Indic language computing on the net?
9. Which T.S. Eliot poem closes with the line 'Shantih Shantih Shantih'?

10. What kind of an animal was Waldi, the first official mascot in the history of the Olympic Games?

11. Ray Tomlinson, who is credited with inventing direct email messages, also popularised which of these symbols?

    a) Hash sign
    b) 'At' sign
    c) Ampersand
    d) Asterisk

12. Miranda and Ariel, the moons of Uranus, are named after characters of which author?

    a) Mark Twain
    b) William Shakespeare
    c) Charles Dickens
    d) Geoffrey Chaucer

WEEK 44

1. Which is the smallest state in India in terms of area?
2. In 1987, which Indian director received the prestigious French Legion of Honor award?
3. Three Nobel Laureates have been under arrest at the time of the award: Carl von Ossietzky, Liu Xiaobo and …
4. Who was the first person from Andhra Pradesh to become the prime minister of India?
5. Which 1955 film starring Raj Kapoor, shares its name with an IPC section?
6. The first Rajdhani Express connected Delhi with which state capital?
7. About whom did Pandit Nehru say, 'He has served his country in many capacities. But above all, he is a great teacher'?
8. Which iconic character did Bobby Kooka and Umesh Rao design initially for memo pads?

9. Balram Halwai is the hero of which Man Booker Prize-winning book?
10. In 2003, India launched the world's largest immunization campaign against which disease?
11. Who among these has played Test cricket for both India and England?
    a) Roger Binny
    b) Iftikhar Ali Khan Pataudi
    c) Vijay Hazare
    d) Farokh Engineer
12. Among the noble gases, which is the most abundant element in the universe?
    a) Xenon
    b) Argon
    c) Helium
    d) Neon

WEEK 45

1. After whose death did Jacques Chirac say, 'This evening, there is less love, less compassion, less light in the world'?
2. Ganesh Bhikaji Deolalikar was the chief architect of which famous building on Tilak Marg, New Delhi?
3. In 1907, who painted *Les Demoiselles d'Avignon*?
4. A PhD Scholarship at St John's College, Cambridge, is named after which former Indian prime minister?
5. Who is the first Bollywood actress to have a wax statue at Madame Tussauds Museum in London?
6. Whose death anniversary is celebrated as Martyr's Day in India?
7. Which was the first Indian company to issue 50- and 100-year bonds in the US debt markets?
8. Which comic-strip character did the French statesman Charles de Gaulle call his 'only international rival'?
9. The official medical term for this is 'lachrymation'. Give me a simpler word for this.

10. What kind of an animal was Shera, the mascot of the 2010 Commonwealth Games?

11. 'Christmas won't be Christmas without any presents,' is the opening line of which novel?

    a) *The Count of Monte Cristo*
    b) *Pride and Prejudice*
    c) *A Christmas Carol*
    d) *Little Women*

12. Which city served as the capital of the United Provinces between 1904 and 1949?

    a) Agra
    b) Allahabad
    c) Kanpur
    d) Benaras

WEEK 46

1. To increase its brilliance, which diamond was cut from 186 one-sixteenth carats to 105.602 carats?
2. In which industrial town was the first Indian Institute of Technology set up?
3. Rolihlahla was the birth name of which Bharat Ratna awardee?
4. Who served as the Minister of Railways in the Union Cabinet from 2004 to 2009?
5. *Fitoor* is the first solo Hindi album of which singer?
6. The world's highest battlefield is located in which glacier?
7. Who has hoisted the National Flag of India 17 consecutive times from the ramparts of the Red Fort?
8. Which city is home to the International Pepper Futures Exchange?
9. In Jules Verne's *Mysterious Island*, which Indian ruler's nephew is Captain Nemo?

10. Who was the first Indian shuttler to clinch a medal at the World Badminton Championships?
11. In the human body, which bone is also known as the 'anvil'?
    a) Scapula
    b) Patella
    c) Tibia
    d) Incus
12. Dalmatian and Rosy are the species of which bird found in India?
    a) Pelican
    b) Eagle
    c) Sparrow
    d) Kingfisher

WEEK 47

1. In 1829, Major R. Smith restored which Indian monument?
2. Which Hindu festival is also known as Surya Shashti?
3. Who was awarded the Nobel Prize for Literature in 2001?
4. Till the Supreme Court of India moved to its present building, which building did it function from?
5. Which actress played the role of Radhika Mathur in the TV series *Hum Paanch*?
6. The Hussain Sagar Lake in Hyderabad has whose monolithic statue in the middle of the lake?
7. The Bibi Ka Maqbara was built to honour which Mughal emperor's wife?
8. The restructuring exercise of which company was dubbed 'Operation Phoenix'?
9. Who received the Sahitya Akademi Award in 1988 for his novel in verse, *The Golden Gate*?
10. Pandora and Phoebe are the moons of which planet in our solar system?

11. The famous programmer, Ada Lovelace, was the daughter of which poet?

    a) Lord Byron
    b) William Wordsworth
    c) P. B. Shelly
    d) John Keats

12. The Dachigam National Park is the habitat of which of these animals?

    a) Asiatic lion
    b) Hangul
    c) Wild ass
    d) Nilgiri tahr

WEEK 48

1. Who, apart from S. Radhakrishnan and C. Rajagopalachari, was awarded the Bharat Ratna in 1954?
2. Hillcroft, an ethnic enclave in Houston, has been renamed after which Indian?
3. Which Indian finance minister changed the budget timings to 11 a.m. in 1999?
4. Park Jae Sang is better known by which stage name?
5. In 2001, Tirana International Airport was renamed after whom?
6. Who did Akbar commission to write his biography, *Akbarnama*?
7. Which term is used by economists to describe the infiltration of the Euro into non-Euro countries of the European Union?
8. Who is the author of a travelogue named *India: A Million Mutinies Now*?
9. Which is Asia's largest antelope?

10. What is the longest running event entirely on a track at the Olympic Games?
11. In which state is Champaran, the site of the indigo rebellion, situated?
    a) Tripura
    b) Bihar
    c) Assam
    d) Madhya Pradesh
12. The device Charles Brannock invented is used to …
    a) Purify blood
    b) Measure feet
    c) Weigh gold
    d) Measure air pressure

WEEK 49

1. In the *Mahabharata*, who was Nakula and Sahadeva's mother?
2. Which food manufacturer claims to have invented the rava idli?
3. On whose birth anniversary on 12 May is International Nurses Day celebrated?
4. Who is the first Parsi member of the House of Lords?
5. In 1976, who became the first Indian film star to be featured on the cover of *TIME* magazine?
6. Inside which UNESCO World Heritage site in Bangladesh would one find Hiron Point, Katka and Tin Kona island?
7. Which is the first Indian product to obtain the Geographical Indications tag?
8. Who wrote the introduction to the English translation of Rabindranath Tagore's *Gitanjali*?
9. Which is the most common subspecies of tiger?

10. In India, the members of which two bodies play cricket for the Raghu Ramaiah Trophy?

11. The first monorail of India was inaugurated in which city?

    a) Bengaluru
    b) Mumbai
    c) Chennai
    d) Kolkata

12. Emma Lazarus wrote *The New Colossus* to help raise money for the ...

    a) Leaning Tower of Pisa
    b) Grand Canyon National Park
    c) Statue of Liberty
    d) Eiffel Tower

WEEK 50

1. In which state is the famous Darjeeling tea grown?
2. In 2008, which Indian sportsperson defeated Leonid Spiridonov to win an Olympic bronze medal?
3. Who was the first English language writer to receive the Nobel Prize for Literature?
4. Who was the first woman nominated as a member of the Rajya Sabha?
5. For which film did Kajol win her first Filmfare Award for Best Actress?
6. The names of 70,000 Indian soldiers are inscribed on the walls of which monument designed by Edwin Lutyens?
7. Who along with Shah Rukh Khan became the first Indian movie star to ring the opening bell in the New York Stock Exchange?
8. Which boy, created by Hank Ketcham, has been '5 an' a half' since he was first created in 1950?

9. After over 20,000 Indian requests, which national symbol was added to FarmVille?
10. Who was awarded the Ramon Magsaysay Award for Emergent Leadership in 2006?
11. Which film ends with a title reading, 'Chris Kyle was killed that day by a veteran he was trying to help'?
    a) *Inglourious Basterds*
    b) *Black Hawk Down*
    c) *American Sniper*
    d) *Fury*
12. Akita, Maltese and Border Collie are breeds of …
    a) Dog
    b) Penguin
    c) Elephant
    d) Ostrich

WEEK 51

1. 'Fidelity, Bravery, Integrity' is the motto of which governmental agency of the United States of America?
2. Who was the first prime minister of India to receive the Bharat Ratna?
3. In *2 States*, what is akin to 'spotting a polar bear in Delhi'?
4. Which sarod maestro composed Raga Priyadarshini in memory of Indira Gandhi?
5. Which festival was known as Eid-e-Gulabi during Shah Jahan's reign?
6. Which famous explorer's autobiography is titled *Nothing Venture, Nothing Win*?
7. In which country is the Komodo National Park located?
8. On whose behalf did Alexander and Kim Aris accept the Nobel Peace Prize in 1991?
9. How many languages are there on the language panel of contemporary currency notes of India?

10. Who bowled the first ball in men's cricket World Cup history?
11. Bhut Jolokia is a type of ...
    a) Lemon
    b) Fish
    c) Chilli
    d) Rice
12. Which bird would you find on the Coat of Arms of South Africa?
    a) Hawk
    b) Starling
    c) Harpy eagle
    d) Secretary

WEEK 52

1. To offset for CO_2 loss, the band Coldplay bought mango trees for villagers in which state in India?
2. Which fictional character has nephews named Huey, Dewey and Louie?
3. Which Hindi film, directed by Vikramaditya Motwane, was inspired by O. Henry's short story *The Last Leaf*?
4. In 1957, which Indian politician gave an eight-hour-long speech at the UN?
5. Who was the first woman to climb Mount Everest?
6. Till 2015, who has played the most IPL matches as captain of his team?
7. The name of which voice-over-Internet Protocol service was derived from the expression 'sky peer-to-peer'?
8. How many stars appear on the flag of China?
9. *Allium cepa* is the scientific name of which vegetable?
10. Which disease is also called 'Breakbone Fever'?

11. Raven is the national bird of which neighbouring country of India?
    a) Nepal
    b) Pakistan
    c) Bhutan
    d) Sri Lanka
12. At the 2010 Oscars, who became the first woman to win in the Best Director category?
    a) Anne Fontaine
    b) Katheryn Bigelow
    c) Gillian Armstrong
    d) Sofia Coppola

BONUS 1

1. *The Revolution* and *Race and People* are two chapters of which famous German's autobiography?
2. Yudhishthira gave Gurgaon to which guru as gurudakshina?
3. Expand the abbreviation POP, used in the world of retail.
4. Who played the role of Amitabh Bachchan's father in the 1985 action film *Mard*?
5. Who was the first finance minister to become the President of India?
6. The Indira Gandhi Wildlife Sanctuary is the largest sanctuary in which state of India?
7. Which animal connects the 1988 Summer Olympic Games, Bangladesh and a novel by Aravind Adiga?
8. Capri pants, a type of close-fitting tapered trousers for women are named after an island off the west coast of which country?
9. Of the six principal organs of the UN, which is the only one to have its seat outside New York, USA?

10. Who is the first cricketer to have taken a hat-trick in Twenty20 Internationals?

BONUS 2

1. Which Nobel Laureate wrote the book *In Light of India*?
2. After independence, in which sport did India win its first individual Olympic medal?
3. In 1932, the first census of which animal was conducted in the Palamau Reserve?
4. In the Indian Navy, the best all-round cadet is awarded with a pair of what?
5. In memory of which former prime minister did Ustad Amjad Ali Khan compose Raga Kamalashree?
6. How is Jorge Mario Bergoglio popularly known to us?
7. Which is the largest internal organ in the human body?
8. In 1986, who wrote a thesis titled *Asset Prices in a Heterogeneous Consumer Economy* at Columbia University?
9. On whose work is the 2002 film *Devdas* based?
10. Located 8 km northwest of Puducherry, what building was designed by architect Roger Anger?

BONUS 3

1. *The Polyester Prince*, written by Hamish McDonald, is an unauthorized biography of whom?
2. The ghoomar dance comes from which Indian state?
3. By what name is the 'swamp deer' popularly known?
4. Who is the first person to win both the Dronacharya Award and the Arjuna Award?
5. If you are visiting the Jaganmohan Palace, Brindavan Garden and Chamundi Hill, which Indian state would you be in?
6. Which ticker symbol does Twitter use on the New York Stock Exchange?
7. Who was the first India-born writer to receive the Nobel Prize for Literature?
8. Which fruit connects a town in Australia, a variety called Cavendish and a 1971 film by Woody Allen?
9. The 4th battalion of the Sikh Light Infantry was the last army unit to be stationed in which UNESCO World

Heritage site in Delhi?

10. *The Periplus*, a manuscript on navigation, called which river 'Nammadus'?

ANSWERS

WEEK 1

1. The Central Bureau of Investigation (CBI) (It traces its origin to the Special Police Establishment which was set up in 1941 by the Government of India.)
2. Agartala (It is the capital of Tripura.)
3. Dr S. Radhakrishnan
4. Hrithik Roshan
5. Saraswati
6. Queen Victoria (William IV, the previous monarch, lived at Clarence House and used St James's Palace for State functions.)
7. Muhurat
8. Rabindranath Tagore
9. Michael Faraday (In 1831, Michael Faraday discovered electromagnetic induction. He gave his name to the 'farad' which later described a unit of electrical capacitance.)

10. His nickname, Sunny
11. *Gone with the Wind*
12. Pizza

WEEK 2

1. Arunachal Pradesh (The population density is 17 persons per sq. km.)
2. Banana
3. Earl Grey
4. Devika Rani (The Government of India conferred on Devika Rani the first Dadasaheb Phalke Award for her outstanding service to the film industry on 21 November 1970.)
5. Afghanistan (The boundary was marked in the Hindu Kush in 1893. Approximately 7.5 million Pashtuns were living in the area around the Durand Line in 1980.)
6. The Battle of Plassey (The British forces under Robert Clive defeated the Nawab of Bengal, Siraj-ud-Dawlah.)
7. Colgate
8. *A Flight of Pigeons* (The film released in 1978. It won the National Film Awards for Best Feature Film, Best Cinematography and Best Audiography.)
9. Gir National Park (It is located in Gujarat.)
10. Alex Ferguson (He served as the team manager for the football club, Manchester United, for 27 years.)
11. Amazon

12. Capri

WEEK 3

1. Sonepur, Bihar (It is one of the largest cattle fairs in India.)
2. Arunachal Pradesh (It has an area of 83,743 sq. km.)
3. Three (Namibia, Niger and Nigeria.)
4. Sardar Vallabhbhai Patel
5. Amitabh Bachchan (Khwaja Ahmad Abbas directed this 1969 film.)
6. Japan
7. Pakistan (It is located in the modern-day Larkana district of Sindh province in Pakistan.)
8. N.R. Narayana Murthy (Narayana Murthy co-founded Infosys.)
9. Typewriter (In 1714, the first typewriter patent known to have been issued, went to an Englishman named Henry Mill.)
10. Australian Open (The Australian Open is the first of the four annual Grand Slam events, played every year in the month of January.)
11. Facsimile
12. Dante Alighieri

WEEK 4

1. Mysore
2. The number, 13

3. Sirimavo Bandaranaike (She created history by becoming the first woman prime minister in the world.)
4. *Yes Minister*
5. Mount Everest (The peak was named after British surveyor George Everest in 1865 and it is the highest mountain in the world.)
6. Reverend Martin Luther King Jr
7. Etihad Airways
8. *A Suitable Boy*
9. Einstein's brain (In 1921, Albert Einstein was awarded the Nobel Prize for Physics.)
10. Anil Kumble
11. Al Gore
12. Italy

WEEK 5

1. English
2. Lotus (The Bahai temple in Delhi is shaped like a lotus. The stems of the lotus flower is used for making Nadroo Kebab. Rajiv is another word for lotus. *Nelumbo nucipera* [Gaertn] is the botanical name of the lotus.)
3. Arrow
4. *Gandhi* (Ben Kingsley played the role of Mahatma Gandhi in this film.)
5. Nepal
6. Golconda Fort (It is located in the western part of

Hyderabad and was originally known as Mankal. Built in 1143, it was originally a mud fort under the reign of the Raja of Warangal.)

7. Deepak Chopra
8. Abhinav Bindra (He became the first individual from India to win an Olympic gold medal when he bagged one at the 2008 Beijing Olympics in the 10-metre air rifle tournament.)
9. Aryabhata (The satellite, Aryabhata's, image appeared on the reverse of Indian two-rupee banknotes between 1976 and 1997.)
10. 60 (In 1975, the first Cricket World Cup was contested in England.)
11. Elisha Otis
12. Spider

WEEK 6

1. Jaipur
2. Hangman's rope
3. Eagle (It appears on the white band of the flag.)
4. Maulana Abul Kalam Azad
5. Ho Chi Minh (Saigon is a city in Vietnam in southeastern Asia.)
6. Swami Vivekananda (Swami Vivekananda left for the US from Bombay (Mumbai) on 31 May 1893.)
7. VRS/Voluntary Retirement Scheme

8. Alberuni
9. Basenji (The Basenji is native to Central Africa.)
10. Armadillo
11. Discworld
12. Turmeric

WEEK 7

1. Maharashtra
2. Napoleon Bonaparte
3. C
4. Rabri Devi (Lalu Pasad Yadav and Rabri Devi have seven daughters and two sons.)
5. *Bombay Talkies* (Each short film was directed by a different director. Zoya Akhtar, Dibakar Banerjee, Karan Johar and Anurag Kashyap were the respective directors.)
6. Haryana
7. JCT
8. Anne Frank (In 1947 her diary was published as *The Diary of a Young Girl,* originally in Dutch.)
9. Knee joint
10. Tamil Nadu
11. Kenya
12. Aardvark

WEEK 8

1. Raman Effect (C.V. Raman was awarded the Nobel Prize in 1930 for his discovery of the 'Raman Effect'.)
2. Rajiv Gandhi
3. Number 8 (At the 2008 Olympic Games, Michael Phelps became the first athlete to win eight gold medals at a single Olympics event. A spider has eight legs. In astrology, Scorpio is the eighth sign of the zodiac.)
4. Morarji Desai (He was born on 29 February 1896 in Bhadeli village, now in the Bulsar district of Gujarat.)
5. Ravi Shankar (Ravi Shankar was nominated for the Academy Awards for the film *Gandhi* in 1983.)
6. Blue Moon
7. Saffron (Saffron is cultivated mainly in Sicily, Spain, France, Italy, Iran and Kashmir, India.)
8. Benares/Varanasi
9. Jupiter (Galileo Galilei built his first telescope in 1609, which let him observe and describe the moons of Jupiter.)
10. Tour de France (Tour de France is the most prestigious bicycle race in the world and it is held for three weeks each year in July.)
11. Sambalpuri
12. Greece

WEEK 9

1. Unique Identification Number (She received it in 2010.)
2. Potato

3. Snake (The staff with the snake has long been a symbol of medicine and the medical profession.)
4. Abhishek Manu Singhvi (His father was L.M. Singhvi.)
5. Danny Denzongpa (Eventually, the role of Gabbar was played by Amjad Khan.)
6. Manipur
7. Singapore (He named the island settlement 'Singapura'. The term means 'Lion City'; 'singa' means lion and 'pura' means city in Sanskrit.)
8. *Sea of Poppies*
9. Alan Shepard (He was the first American in space and he became the first person to hit a golf ball on the moon.)
10. Arjun Atwal
11. Tethering
12. Lata Mangeshkar

WEEK 10

1. Indian Navy
2. Tamil Nadu (Kollywood is derived from 'Kodambakkam' in Chennai.)
3. Russia
4. Grover Cleveland (He served as President in 1885–89 and again in 1893–97.)
5. Pitbull (He was born on 14 January 1981 in Miami, USA.)
6. Kamakhya Temple

7. Qutb Minar (The foundation of the Qutb Minar was laid by Qutb-ud-Din Aibak in AD 1199.)
8. Alyque Padamsee
9. Crows
10. Galileo Galilei
11. James Parkinson
12. Banjo

WEEK 11

1. Republic Day (Padma Awards are conferred in three categories, namely, the Padma Vibhushan, Padma Bhushan and Padma Shri. The Awards are given for contribution in various fields of activities including art, social work, public affairs, science and engineering.)
2. Rose (Hybrid tea is a class of Rose. Kate Winslet's name in *Titanic* was Rose DeWitt Bukater and *The Name of the Rose* is a book by Umberto Eco.)
3. Leader of the Opposition
4. Dilip Kumar (Dilip Kumar was born on 11 December 1922. He is famous for his roles in films like *Devdas*, *Andaz*, *Mughal-e-Azam*, among others)
5. Sri Lanka
6. Jayadeva
7. Only Vimal/Vimal
8. Dilbert (The comic strip *Dilbert* is illustrated by Scott Adams.)

9. Venus
10. Baichung Bhutia (He has captained the Indian football team.)
11. Domain
12. Strawberry

WEEK 12

1. National Flag
2. Central Bureau of Investigation
3. Indonesia
4. Vice-President of India
5. *Sarfarosh* (*Sarfarosh* was released in 1999 and Sonali Bendre was the lead actress in the film.)
6. The Hague
7. Alexander the Great
8. C.K. Prahalad
9. Isaac Newton (He discovered gravity and the laws of motion and invented calculus.)
10. England
11. Power
12. Munshi Premchand

WEEK 13

1. Rajdhani Express
2. April (The financial year of India starts from 1 April and

ends on 31 March.)

3. International Committee of the Red Cross (1917, 1944 and 1963.)
4. Indira Gandhi
5. Lata Mangeshkar
6. Krishna
7. Haryana
8. Feni (Feni liquor is made from cashew apples in Goa.)
9. Geneva
10. Basketball (Jennifer Paes went on to captain the national team in 1982.)
11. Rajasthan
12. Andes

WEEK 14

1. Delhi
2. The *Ramayana* (C. Rajagopalachari received the Sahitya Akademi Award for his retelling of the *Ramayana*, Valmiki, author of the *Ramayana* is regarded as the Adi Kavi and Shatrughan Sinha's house in Mumbai is called 'Ramayan'.)
3. Olive
4. Sharmila Tagore (Rajesh Khanna was the lead actor in this film, which won three Filmfare awards in 1970.)
5. Suez Canal (It runs across the Isthmus of Suez in Egypt to connect the Mediterranean and the Red Seas. The Suez Canal separates Africa from Asia.)

6. Shams-ud-Din Iltutmish (He was the son-in-law of Qutb-ud-Din Aibak and succeeded him in 1211.)
7. Operation Flood/White Revolution (The White Revolution consisted of three phases; the last phase ended in 1996.)
8. Fox Terrier (In French, Snowy is called Milou.)
9. Kalpana Chawla (She was the first Indian–American astronaut and first Indian woman in space.)
10. P.T. Usha (P.T. Usha is an Indian track and field athlete who has represented India in the Olympics and many other international sporting events.)
11. Citizenship
12. Capillary

WEEK 15

1. 2 October
2. Rabindranath Tagore
3. Manmohan Singh (He signed the banknotes in his capacity as the Governor of the Reserve Bank of India, a position he held from 16 September 1982 to 14 January 1985.)
4. Kamal Haasan (Kamal Haasan and Tabu were the lead actors in this 1997 film.)
5. Darjeeling (Darjeeling is located in the state of West Bengal.)
6. Bal Gangadhar Tilak (He founded the Indian Home Rule League in 1914 and served as its president.)
7. Buy One Get One Free

8. Grand Trunk Road
9. Pope Francis I (The tweet, when roughly translated from Latin, means 'We have Pope Francis')
10. Waqar Younis, who also made his test debut in the same match.
11. Rock
12. Adolf Hitler

WEEK 16

1. Jharkhand
2. Use it in the kitchen of the temple as firewood to cook prasad
3. Gold (Charlie Chaplin acted in a film named *The Gold Rush*. Pyrite is also called Fool's Gold. The discovery of gold nuggets in the Sacramento Valley of California in the 1800s is said to have sparked the Gold Rush.)
4. Jawaharlal Nehru (The no-confidence motion was moved in August of 1963.)
5. Shah Rukh Khan
6. Ganga
7. Snapchat
8. Jawaharlal Nehru (He became the first prime minister of India.)
9. Chihuahua (It is named after a state in Northern Mexico.)
10. Red ring (The Olympic rings represent the union of the five continents and the meeting of athletes from around

the world at the Olympic Games.)

11. Response
12. Mountain range

WEEK 17

1. Maharashtra (It is held along the banks of the Godavari river in Nashik. It is believed to be one of the largest gatherings of people for a religious purpose in the world.)
2. Sikkim
3. Mona Lisa
4. Vilasrao Deshmukh
5. *Dabangg* (A sequel to this film, *Dabangg 2*, was released in 2012.)
6. Arunachal Pradesh
7. Charkha
8. Diamond
9. Khushwant Singh (He was born in 1915 in Hadali (now in Pakistan). He was a member of the Rajya Sabha from 1980 to 1986 and was awarded the Padma Bhushan in 1974 by the President of India.)
10. Lord's
11. Bharat Vidhata
12. Muhammed Ali Jinnah

WEEK 18

1. Kuchipudi

2. Louis I. Kahn
3. S. Radhakrishnan (He was the first Chairman of the Rajya Sabha to serve two consecutive terms (13 May 1952 to 12 May 1962.) Mohammad Hamid Ansari served as the Vice-President of India from 11 August 2007 and was re-elected to the post on 7 August 2012
4. *Slumdog Millionaire* (This film won eight Oscar awards and was nominated for two more in 2009.)
5. Kanchenjunga (It is situated in the eastern Himalayas on the border between the state of Sikkim in northeastern India, and eastern Nepal. The mountain is part of the Great Himalayan Range. The five peaks are considered to be treasuries of gold and silver.)
6. Jahangir (He was born as Prince Salim and was the Mughal emperor of India from 1605 to 1627.)
7. Totapuri
8. Kiran Desai (She won the Man Booker Prize for her book *The Inheritance of Loss* in 2006.)
9. Ronald Ross (He won the Nobel Prize for Physiology or Medicine in 1902.)
10. Rugby
11. Nebuliser
12. Scooby Doo

WEEK 19

1. Rock Garden (Nek Chand used waste materials like broken crockery, electrical fittings, glass bangles, bathroom tiles

and washbasins in creating this iconic garden.)

2. Zubin Mehta
3. Pranab Mukherjee
4. *Barfi!* (Ranbir Kapoor and Ileana D'Cruz were the lead actors in this film, which was the Indian entry for the Foreign Language Film in the 2013 Academy Awards.)
5. Karakoram (The Karakoram has Hindu Kush to its west, the Pamirs to the northwest, the Kunlun Mountains to the northeast and the Himalayas to the southeast.)
6. Kohinoor
7. Edward de Bono
8. Lewis Carroll (The novel *Alice's Adventures in Wonderland* by Lewis Carroll was published in 1865 and was illustrated by John Tenniel.)
9. Sabeer Bhatia (They founded Hotmail, a web mail service, in the year 1996 and sold it two years later to Microsoft for a whopping $400 million.)
10. Stuart Broad (Stuart Broad is an English cricketer.)
11. Computer printers
12. Snoopy

WEEK 20

1. Brahmos
2. Mango
3. Nairobi (It is the capital of Kenya.)
4. Dr Rajendra Prasad

5. Sridevi
6. Karnataka (Hampi is situated on the southern bank of the Tungabhadra river. The traditional name of Hampi is Pampakshetra of Kishkindha.)
7. *Guru Granth Sahib*
8. R.K. Laxman (Sales zoomed ten-folds after the introduction of Gattu in 1954. He was accompanied by the line 'Any surface that needs painting needs Asian Paints'.)
9. Malgudi (It is a fictitious town in India created by R.K. Narayan in his novels and short stories.)
10. East Bengal
11. Red
12. Honey Singh

WEEK 21

1. National Security Guards (NSG)
2. Train names in India
3. IIM Ahmedabad
4. France
5. Aishwarya Rai
6. Pakistan
7. Charminar (It is located in the city of Hyderabad. The construction of the Charminar was completed in 1591.)
8. Nirma
9. Fauntleroy

10. Japan
11. Marie Curie
12. Dundee

WEEK 22

1. Kolkata (The National Library in Alipore.)
2. Bhutan
3. V.V. Giri
4. *Rowdy Rathore* (Akshay Kumar and Sonakshi Sinha were the lead actors in this 2012 film and it was directed by Prabhu Deva.)
5. Goa
6. Porus/Poru (Porus was an Indian prince who ruled the region between the Hydaspes (Jhelum) and Acesines (Chenab) rivers at the time of Alexander the Great's invasion of Punjab.)
7. David Ogilvy (In 1948, he founded the New York-based ad agency Hewitt, Ogilvy, Benson & Mather, which eventually became Ogilvy & Mather Worldwide.)
8. Mark Twain (The name Mark Twain is the pen name of Samuel Langhorne Clemens.)
9. Euphoria
10. Suresh Raina
11. Laparoscope
12. Indore

WEEK 23

1. Cherrapunji (It is one of the wettest places on the earth.)
2. Pandit Ravi Shankar
3. Nelson Mandela
4. Kenya
5. Rajesh Khanna
6. Siachen
7. Fatehpur Sikri (It is located in Uttar Pradesh. Akbar shifted his residence and court from Agra to Sikri for a period of 13 years to honour the Sufi saint Sheikh Salim Chishti. Akbar respected him very much as he blessed him with a son.)
8. Maximum City
9. Piranha
10. Sourav Ganguly
11. Human blood transfusion
12. Abraham Lincoln

WEEK 24

1. Ahmedabad in Gujarat
2. King George VI (Colin Firth played the role of the king.)
3. Charan Singh (One of the supporting parties withdrew its support just a few days after he assumed office on 28 July 1979 and he continued as caretaker prime minister till fresh elections were held.)

4. Jammu and Kashmir (The word 'waz' means chef and 'wan' denotes an array of meat curries and other dishes.)
5. Bangladesh (The boundary stretches for about 4056 km, out of which 2216.7 km lie in West Bengal.)
6. Mother Teresa (Mother Teresa was born as Agnes Gonxha Bojaxhiu in Skopje, Macedonia.)
7. Raj Krishna (He coined the term for India's low rate of GDP growth between the 1950s and 1980s.)
8. Mowgli (Mowgli is a character from Rudyard Kipling's *The Jungle Book*.)
9. Merry Christmas
10. Milkha Singh
11. Refrigerator
12. Mother India

WEEK 25

1. Norah Jones
2. Snakes and Ladders
3. Pakistan
4. Sir Winston Churchill
5. Anurag Kashyap
6. Ganga
7. Jai Hind
8. Hinduja Group
9. Anaconda

10. South Africa
11. Cache
12. Nepal

WEEK 26

1. Tripura
2. Srinivasan Ramanujan (He was born in 1887.)
3. Literature
4. Kofi Annan (He served as the seventh Secretary-General of the UN.)
5. Irrfan Khan
6. Ranjit Singh
7. Shobha De
8. Padma Patil
9. Kaziranga
10. Billiards
11. Timeline
12. Mahadev Desai

WEEK 27

1. M.F. Husain
2. Neem
3. Apple (*The Apple Cart* is a play by G.B. Shaw. Golden Delicious is a variety of apple. The Beatles founded Apple Records in 1968.)

4. Mansur Ali Khan Pataudi
5. *Taare Zameen Par*
6. Jog Falls/Gersoppa Falls/Joga Falls (It is a cataract of the Sharavati river in the western part of Karnataka state. It plunges 830 feet and splits into four cascades known as the Raja, Roarer, Rocket and Ranee.)
7. Charminar (The term 'Charminar' comes from two words 'char' and 'minar', which means four towers.)
8. Hyderabad (Facebook started its India operation in 2010 and the office in Hyderabad is also the first office of Facebook in Asia.)
9. Ruskin Bond
10. Great Dane
11. Ho Chi Minh
12. An Indian woman summitted Mount Everest

WEEK 28

1. Holi
2. Mother Teresa
3. The Pope (It is a part of his regalia. Originally, the Fisherman's Ring was a signet which was used to seal official documents signed by the Pope.)
4. Pratibha Patil (She served as President of India from 25 July 2007 to 25 July 2012.)
5. *Titanic* (The film won 11 Oscar awards and was nominated for three more. The lead actors in the movie were Leonardo

di Caprio and Kate Winslet. 'My Heart Will Go On' sung by Celine Dion, is a popular song from this film.)

6. Karnataka
7. Sher Shah Suri
8. Naresh Goyal
9. Phileas Fogg
10. Churchill Brothers
11. Leonardo da Vinci
12. Tea

WEEK 29

1. Kathak
2. George Harrison
3. Australia
4. Manmohan Singh (He served as prime minister from 22 May 2004 to 26 May 2014.)
5. Dev Anand
6. Qutb Minar
7. Akbar (He ruled from 1556 to 1605 and extended Mughal power over most of the Indian subcontinent.)
8. Picnic
9. Manipur
10. New Zealand
11. Nelson Mandela
12. Liver

WEEK 30

1. Zakir Hussain
2. Kalyug
3. A.P.J. Abdul Kalam
4. Dadasaheb Phalke
5. Hawa Mahal, Jaipur (This palace was constructed in 1799 by Maharaja Sawai Pratap Singh who belonged to the Kachhwaha Rajput dynasty. The palace is mainly built of red and pink sandstone.)
6. Kautilya's *Arthasastra* (Kautilya is also known as Chanakya or Vishnugupta. He was the counsellor and adviser to Chandragupta Maurya.)
7. Ogilvy and Mather
8. Popeye (Elzie Segar introduced Popeye in a 1929 comic strip.)
9. Gujarat
10. Leander Paes
11. Neptune
12. Joe Root

WEEK 31

1. George Harrison
2. Amartya Sen
3. Allama Iqbal
4. Shammi Kapoor (Shammi Kapoor, Sanjeev Kumar and

Zeenat Aman were the lead actors in the film.)

5. Tahrir Square
6. Rashtrapati Bhavan (The architect of the Rashtrapati Bhavan was Edwin Landseer Lutyens and it was the erstwhile residence of the British Viceroy.)
7. Carpet
8. R.K. Laxman (In 2005, he was awarded the Padma Vibhushan. He was also honoured with the Ramon Magsaysay Award for Journalism, Literature and Creative Communication Arts in 1984.)
9. Bombay
10. Jacques Kallis (Jacques Kallis is a South African cricketer.)
11. Mahatma Gandhi
12. Elephanta Caves

WEEK 32

1. India Post
2. Taj Mahal (The other wonders' on the list are: Christ the Redeemer, Machu Picchu, Chichén Itzá, the Colosseum, Petra, the Great Wall of China.)
3. Cambodia (The temple is dedicated to Lord Shiva.)
4. Nelson Mandela (He received it in 1990.)
5. M.F. Husain
6. Gol Gumbaz (Soon after he came to the throne in 1626, Muhammad Adil Shah started constructing this structure to bury his mortal remains. He was buried in the vast

vault beneath the floor along with other family members.)

7. Christopher Columbus (In 1492, he sailed from Europe to America but he was not the one to discover America as many people were already living there.)
8. Rabindranath Tagore
9. Kaziranga (It is located in Assam.)
10. Pete Sampras
11. Forest conservation
12. Tipu Sultan

WEEK 33

1. Elephant
2. Grapes
3. Sri Lanka
4. Indira Gandhi (She presented the budget for the year 1970–71.)
5. Dilip Kumar
6. Rumi Darwaza/Turkish Gateway
7. Nadir Shah
8. Philips (It is the sound-and-light show whereby multicoloured lights are directed against the façade of the Red Fort. The changes of light are synchronized with a sound track.)
9. Ray Bradbury (His first book of short stories was *Dark Carnival* which was published in 1947.)
10. Sir Vivian Richards

11. Moa
12. An earthen pot

WEEK 34

1. Sumantra Ghoshal (He was the Professor of Strategic and International Management at the London Business School, and was the founding Dean of the Indian School of Business, Hyderabad.)
2. Eiffel Tower (The total elevation of the tower is 324 metres, including the height of the tower, the base and the television antenna.)
3. The President
4. Subhash Ghai
5. Taj Mahal (It is situated in Uttar Pradesh, along the banks of the Yamuna river. Taj Mahal was built by the Mughal emperor Shah Jahan in memory of his wife Mumtaz Mahal.)
6. Tipu Sultan's sword (Vijay Mallya bought the sword in 2003 and it was re-sold in 2010 for a record 505,250 pounds.)
7. Parliament building
8. Republic
9. Snakes
10. The Oval (It hosted its first Test cricket tournament in 1880.)
11. Antarctica
12. Hattie McDaniel

WEEK 35

1. Wendell Rodricks
2. Rajasthan
3. Teddy bear (Morris Michtom, along with his wife, created the first Teddy bear. Teddy is Mr Bean's life-long best friend. The British broadcaster Gyles Brandreth founded a Teddy Bear Museum in Stratford-upon-Avon.)
4. Queen Elizabeth II
5. *Slumdog Millionaire*
6. Qutb Minar
7. Harshavardhana (He was the ruler of a large empire in northern India in 606–47 CE)
8. Richie Rich
9. China
10. Sunil Chhetri
11. Tuberculosis
12. Jack Kilby

WEEK 36

1. Gujarat (The fair is held a fortnight after Holi, around the month of March–April. It starts on the eve of the new moon (called Amavas), the time when the wheat crop is ready for harvest.)
2. Nepal (It is in Kathmandu.)
3. The President

4. Christian Bale
5. Sri Lanka
6. Babur (The original name of Babur is Zahir al-Din Muhammad. He was the founder of the Mughal dynasty of India.)
7. WagonR (The mascot aimed to represent everything that the brand WagonR stands for, like smartness and leadership.)
8. Roald Dahl (Roald Dahl's first novel, consciously written for children, was *James and the Giant Peach*, which was launched in 1961.)
9. Jim Corbett (The Jim Corbett National Park is located in Uttarakhand.)
10. Chris Gayle
11. Jagadish Chandra Bose
12. Further Beyond

WEEK 37

1. Pratibha Patil, the then President
2. Supreme Court of India
3. New York
4. The President of India
5. Priyanka Chopra
6. Netaji Subhas Chandra Bose International Airport, Kolkata
7. Red Fort (Construction of the Red Fort began on 13 May 1638 and it was completed in nine years, two months and

some days. 18 April 1648 was chosen as the date for Shah Jahan to shift to his new palace, Quila-i-Surkh[Red Fort].)

8. Abdul Karim Telgi
9. Salim Ali (Salim Ali was the first non-Britisher to win the prestigious gold medal of the British Ornithologist Union in 1967.)
10. Usain Bolt (He is a Jamaican sprinter, who won gold medals at both the Beijing 2008 Olympic Games and the London 2012 Games.)
11. Edwin Hubble
12. Uganda

WEEK 38

1. Rabindranath Tagore
2. Odisha
3. H.D. Gowda (He served as the prime minister of India from 1 June 1996 to 21 April 1997)
4. Akshay Kumar
5. Indonesia
6. Cellular Jail (It is situated on the South Andaman island. Netaji called it the Indian Bastille when he visited it on 29 December 1943.)
7. Amul Butter girl (The Amul Butter girl was created in 1966 and since then appears in the advertisements representing current affairs around the world.)
8. Salman Rushdie (His second novel, *Midnight's Children*,

was published in 1981 and in 1993 it was judged to be the 'Booker of Bookers'.)

9. Malaria (Malaria is caused by parasites that are transmitted to people through the bites of infected mosquitoes.)
10. Javagal Srinath (He has officiated as the ICC match referee in 177 ODIs.)
11. Leaning Tower of Pisa
12. Dalai Lama

WEEK 39

1. Agartala (It was built by Maharaja Radha Kishore Manikya in 1899–1901.)
2. Ahmedabad
3. Brazil (The words mean 'Order and Progress.')
4. The President
5. Chetan Bhagat (The novel is called *One Night at the Call Centre.*)
6. Ooty/Ootacamund/Udhagai/Udhagamandala (Ooty is a town on the Nilgiri Hills in the state of Tamil Nadu.)
7. Boston Tea Party
8. Plague
9. Salt
10. Australian Open
11. Simon
12. Robin

WEEK 40

1. Telephone directory
2. Uttarakhand
3. Barack Obama (He received it for for his extraordinary efforts to strengthen international diplomacy and cooperation between peoples.)
4. Neelam S. Reddy (He served as the President of India from 25 July 1977 to 25 July 1982.)
5. Shah Rukh Khan ('Red Chillies Entertainment' was founded in 2002 in Mumbai.)
6. Delhi
7. Ibn Battuta
8. Child Rights and You (Rippan Kapur, a young airline purser, founded this NGO in the 1970s. The acronym formerly stood for 'Child Relief and You')
9. New Zealand
10. Virender Sehwag (He has scored 91 sixes)
11. Gallbladder
12. Lady Gaga

WEEK 41

1. Land of Seven Sisters
2. William Shakespeare (In 1964.)
3. Richard Nixon (He was the 37th President of the United States of America.)

4. Piscine Molitor Patel (Pi) (He is the central character of the 2012 film *Life of Pi*. The film won four Oscar Awards and was nominated for seven more in 2013.)
5. Palace on Wheels (Every Wednesday, the luxury train commences on its week-long journey between Delhi and Jaipur, including a trip also to Agra and the Taj Mahal.)
6. Bara Imambara (The architect Kifayatullah designed it. He is said to be a relative of the architect of the Taj Mahal. The construction of the Bara Imambara was completed in 11 years and was ready in 1795.)
7. SpiceJet (Mustard, Tamarind and Sesame Chilli, Garlic, Heeng, etc. are the names of some of the other aircrafts run by SpiceJet.)
8. Selfie (According to the Oxford Dictionaries, the definition of a 'selfie' is: 'A photograph that one has taken of oneself, typically one taken with a smartphone or webcam and shared via social media'.)
9. Emu
10. Cristiano Ronaldo
11. Black Widow
12. Europe

WEEK 42

1. Pune (Ahmednagar is the largest)
2. Religious workers
3. Jimmy Carter (He visited the village when he came to India in 1978. It's called Carterpuri.)

4. *Lekin*
5. Uttar Pradesh
6. Rani Lakshmibai of Jhansi
7. Maruti 800 (He bought the car in 1983 for Rs 47,500 and the keys of the car was handed to him by Indira Gandhi, the prime minister back then.)
8. Spiderman/Peter Parker (Peter Parker was raised by his elderly Uncle Ben and Aunt May. At the age of 15, he was bitten by a radioactive spider on the hand which gave him the strength and agility of an arachnid.)
9. Walked on the moon (John Young has flown two Gemini missions in the earth's orbit and flown twice to the moon, although he only landed once, on Apollo 16; James Irwin landed on the moon with Dave Scott in 1971; Alan Bean and Pete Conrad landed in a region of the moon called the Ocean of Storms in 1969.)
10. A.R. Rahman (The 2010 Commonwealth Games was held in Delhi.)
11. Wild Draw Four
12. Personal computer

WEEK 43

1. Buddha
2. Darjeeling tea
3. J.R.D. Tata
4. Indira Gandhi (It is located in Delhi.)

5. *Yamla Pagla Deewana*
6. Kanha National Park
7. Swami Vivekananda (He was born as Narendranath Datta in Calcutta (Kolkata) on 12 January 1863. The Government of India has been celebrating 12 January as National Youth Day since 1984.)
8. Microsoft
9. *The Waste Land* (The poem is a very long one and was edited by Ezra Pound who helped condense the original to nearly half its size.)
10. Dog (Waldi was introduced in the 1972 Munich Olympic Games. Waldi was born on 15 December 1969 at a Munich Games Organizing Committee Christmas party.)
11. 'At' sign
12. William Shakespeare

WEEK 44

1. Goa
2. Satyajit Ray
3. Aung San Suu Kyi
4. P.V. Narasimha Rao (He served as prime minister from 21 June 1991 to 16 May 1996.)
5. *Shree 420*
6. Kolkata
7. S. Radhakrishnan (Dr Radhakrishnan was elected Vice-President in 1952 and in 1962, he was elected President

for a period of five years. His birthday is celebrated as Teachers' Day in India.)

8. The Air India Maharaja
9. *The White Tiger* (Aravind Adiga won the Man Booker Prize for *The White Tiger* in 2008.)
10. Polio (In 2014, India was certified as polio-free by the World Health Organization.)
11. Iftikhar Ali Khan Pataudi
12. Helium

WEEK 45

1. Mother Teresa (She passed away on 5 September 1997.)
2. Supreme Court of India
3. Pablo Picasso
4. Dr Manmohan Singh
5. Aishwarya Rai Bachchan (Her wax statue was installed in the year 2004.)
6. Mahatma Gandhi (Every year on 30 January, the nation pays homage to the Mahatma and other martyrs.)
7. Reliance Industries Ltd (RIL) (Dhirubhai Ambani founded this company in 1966.)
8. Tintin (Tintin was created in 1929 by Georges Remi, Hergé, a Belgian cartoonist.)
9. Crying/Weeping
10. Tiger
11. *Little Women*

12. Allahabad

WEEK 46

1. Kohinoor
2. Kharagpur (It is located in West Bengal.)
3. Nelson Mandela
4. Lalu Prasad Yadav (Lalu Prasad Yadav presented the railway budget six times in a row, from 2004 to May 2009.)
5. Mohit Chauhan
6. Siachen Glacier (Siachen Glacier is one of the world's longest mountain glaciers. It lies in the Karakoram Range system in Kashmir.)
7. Jawaharlal Nehru (His daughter Indira Gandhi had unfurled the flag 11 consecutive times between 1966 and 1977.)
8. Kochi
9. Tipu Sultan
10. Prakash Padukone (Copenhagen, 1983.)
11. Incus
12. Pelican

WEEK 47

1. Qutb Minar
2. Chhath Puja (It is dedicated to the Hindu sun god, Surya.)
3. V.S. Naipaul

4. Parliament House (The inauguration of the Supreme Court of India took place in the Chamber of Princes in the Parliament building.)
5. Vidya Balan
6. Gautama Buddha
7. Aurangzeb (Prince Azam Shah is believed to have constructed the mausoleum in memory of his mother.)
8. Tech Mahindra/Satyam (after a scam) (The operation was named so after the mythical bird that's reborn from its own ashes every time it dies. The operation was categorized into four sections, including laying off, retrenchment and rebranding.)
9. Vikram Seth
10. Saturn
11. Lord Byron
12. Hangul

WEEK 48

1. C.V. Raman
2. Mahatma Gandhi
3. Yashwant Sinha (Before 1999, the General Budget was presented at 5 p.m. on the last working day of February.)
4. PSY (PSY is popular for his song 'Gangnam Style', which surpassed the YouTube view limit in 2014.)
5. Mother Teresa
6. Abul Fazl (Abul Fazl and his elder brother Faizi were the

two of the nine gems of the court of Akbar.)

7. Eurocreep
8. V.S. Naipaul (He was awarded the Nobel Prize for Literature in 2001.)
9. Nilgai
10. 10,000-metre event
11. Bihar
12. Measure feet

WEEK 49

1. Madri
2. MTR
3. Florence Nightingale
4. Karan Faridoon Bilimoria
5. Parveen Babi (Among others, Mahatma Gandhi, Sachin Tendulkar, Aishwariya Rai also featured on the cover of *TIME* magazine.)
6. The Sunderbans
7. Tea
8. W.B. Yeats (The English translation of *Gitanjali*, was instrumental in popularizing Tagore in the West, thereby helping him win the Nobel Prize for Literature in 1913.)
9. Royal Bengal Tiger
10. Lok Sabha vs Rajya Sabha
11. Mumbai

12. Statue of Liberty

WEEK 50

1. West Bengal
2. Sushil Kumar
3. Rudyard Kipling (He received it in 1907.)
4. Rukmini Devi Arundale (A famous classical dancer, she was nominated in the year 1952.)
5. *Dilwale Dulhaniya Le Jayenge*
6. India Gate (The foundation stone of India Gate was laid by the Duke of Connaught in 1921.)
7. Kajol (This event took place in 2010, while Shah Rukh Khan and Kajol were in New York to promote their film *My Name is Khan*.)
8. Dennis the Menace (The character Dennis, created by Hank Ketcham, made his debut on 12 March 1951.)
9. The Indian tricolour
10. Arvind Kejriwal
11. *American Sniper*
12. Dog

WEEK 51

1. Federal Bureau of Investigation (FBI) (The motto is said to have its origin in a brief comment by Inspector W.H. Drane Lester, the editor of the magazine, *The Investigator*, in 1935.)

2. Jawaharlal Nehru (He received the Bharat Ratna in 1955.)
3. A 'sardarji' in Chennai
4. Ustad Amjad Ali Khan
5. Holi
6. Edmund Hillary (He was the first to reach the summit of Mount Everest, the highest mountain in the world.)
7. Indonesia (This national park consists of three major islands, inhabited by a population of giant lizards, whose appearance and aggressive behaviour have led to them being called 'Komodo dragons'. They exist nowhere else in the world.)
8. Aung San Suu Kyi (On 14 October, the Norwegian Nobel Committee announced Suu Kyi as the winner of the 1991 Peace Prize. Her children received the prize on her behalf in Oslo as she was in detention.)
9. Fifteen (The first language to appear on the panel is Assamese and the last to appear is Urdu. The languages are arranged alphabetically.)
10. Madan Lal
11. Chilli
12. Secretary

WEEK 52

1. Karnataka
2. Donald Duck
3. *Lootera* (Ranveer Singh and Sonakshi Sinha played the

lead roles in the 2013 film *Lootera*.)

4. V.K. Krishna Menon (He defended India's position on Kashmir.)
5. Junko Tabei (A Japanese mountaineer, she reached the top on 16 May 1975.)
6. M.S. Dhoni (India won the 50-over ICC World Cup in 2011 and the World Twenty20 in 2007 under his captaincy.)
7. Skype (Founded in 2003, Skype is a part of Microsoft.)
8. Five—one large yellow five-pointed star and four smaller yellow five-pointed stars
9. Onion
10. Dengue (Dengue is transmitted by the bite of a mosquito which has been infected with one of the four dengue virus serotypes.)
11. Bhutan
12. Katheryn Bigelow

BONUS 1

1. Adolf Hitler (Adolf Hitler ruled Germany from 1933 to 1945 and called himself 'Führer' meaning 'the leader'.)
2. Dronacharya
3. Point of Purchase (It involves products displays and other last-minute marketing tactics to influence the customer to choose a specific brand or to make an impulse buy.)
4. Dara Singh
5. R. Venkataraman

6. Tamil Nadu
7. Tiger (The tiger named Hodori was the official mascot of the 1988 Summer Olympics; the Royal Bengal Tiger is the National Animal of Bangladesh; Aravind Adiga won the Man Booker Prize in 2008 for his book *The White Tiger*.)
8. Italy
9. International Court of Justice (The Hague.)
10. Brett Lee (Brett Lee is a former Australian cricketer.)

BONUS 2

1. Octavio Paz (He received the Nobel Prize for Literature in 1990.)
2. Wrestling (In 1952, wrestler K.D. Jadhav became the first Indian to win an individual Olympic medal.)
3. Tiger
4. Binoculars
5. Rajiv Gandhi
6. Pope Francis (He was elected Supreme Pontiff on 13 March 2013.)
7. Liver
8. Vikram Pandit
9. Sarat Chandra Chatterjee (The name, Awara Masiha, was given to Sarat Chandra Chatterjee by the late Hindi litterateur Vishnu Prabhakar who wrote his biography by that name.)

10. Auroville (Conceived by the Mother, it came into existence in 1968.)

BONUS 3

1. Dhirubhai Ambani
2. Rajasthan
3. Barasingha
4. Syed Naeemuddin, the football player and national team coach.
5. Karnataka
6. TWTR
7. Rudyard Kipling (He received the Nobel Prize for Literature in 1907, and was born in Bombay in 1865.)
8. Banana (Banana is a small town in Central Queensland, Australia; Cavendish bananas are categorized as 'dessert bananas'; Woody Allen directed the film *Bananas* in 1971.)
9. Red Fort (It was handed over to the Archaeological Survey of India in December 2003.)
10. Narmada (The river was called Namade by the second century Greek geographer Ptolemy. It rises in the Maikala Range in east-central Madhya Pradesh. Some important cities and towns along its banks are Jabalpur, Hoshangabad and Mandhata.)